S E L E C T E D   P O E M S

John Blight was born in South Australia in 1913 but has spent most of his adult life in Queensland. In 1939, his poems were first published in the *Bulletin*, establishing his long association with Australia's leading literary magazines.

His numerous awards include the 1964 Myer award, with *A Beachcomber's Diary* winning the best Australian book of verse; the 1965 Dame Mary Gilmore Medal; the 1976 Patrick White Award; a National Book Council literary award in 1976 for *Selected Poems 1939-1975*; the Grace Leven Prize for poetry in 1977; and the Christopher Brennan Award in 1980.

He received an emeritus fellowship from the Literature Board in 1984 and an order of merit for services to literature in 1987. John Blight and his wife live in Brisbane.

# John Blight

## SELECTED POEMS
### *1939 • 1990*

University of Queensland Press

First published 1992 by University of Queensland Press
Box 42, St Lucia, Queensland 4067 Australia

Typeset by University of Queensland Press
Printed in Australia by The Book Printer, Victoria


Distributed in the USA and Canada by
International Specialized Book Services, Inc.,
5602 N.E. Hassalo Street, Portland, Oregon 97213-3640

Creative writing program assisted by
the Australia Council, the Australian
Government's arts funding and
advisory body

**Cataloguing in Publication Data**
*National Library of Australia*

Blight, John, 1913-
   John Blight, selected poems 1939-1990.

   I. Title. II. Title: Selected poems 1939-1990.

A821.3

ISBN 0 7022 2425 1

To Claire Ellen Ward

# Contents

From *A Beachcomber's Diary* (1963)

From *My Beachcombing Days* (1968)

From *Pageantry for a Lost Empire* (1977)

Uncollected and Later Poems

# Introduction

John Blight is one of Australia's most remarkable poets. The single word which permeates the essays and reviews devoted to his work is "original", and this adjective can seldom have been better employed than as a summation of the character of his fifty years of poems. A long lifetime of engagement with the writing and publishing of poetry, and the reading of the poetry of his contemporaries, seems to have left almost no mark on his own poetry in terms of influences, though echoes of the distinctive quality of his own work can often be heard in the poetry of his younger contemporaries.

His first poems were written under the influence of nineteenth century English models and his instinctive appreciation at an early age of their failure and his consequent search for a voice which would be his own without being an imitation of contemporary modes was an important literary event in the late thirties and forties. An individual voice also needs a sympathetic home and Blight was fortunate that his distinctive poetry was welcomed at the *Bulletin* then under the first phase of Douglas Stewart's editorship of its literary pages.

Publication in the *Bulletin* did not lead to any flattening out of distinctiveness and Blight was able to pursue his own course with the same calm sense of what was right for him that he has always demonstrated. Stewart was inclined to ask of the poets he published that they try a large, narrative, mythic poem, usually dealing with explorers, as a way of fulfilling one of poetry's traditional functions: to give its culture access to its early experience by myths. Blight had enough sense of his own limitations and strengths to resist this, and when his early poems do approach narrative it is always in a highly allusive and dramatic way — the mode, ultimately, of the lyric.

His first publication in the *Bulletin* in 1939 occurred in his twenty-sixth year. His life until then had been spent largely in

Queensland. His parents had moved to the Brisbane area from South Australia when Blight was an infant, and Blight's father was a real estate agent with his own office, a lover of sport and horse racing, able to provide a comfortable life for his family. Blight left school in the eleventh grade and did odd-jobs as well as completing accountancy qualifications. In the mid-thirties he spent some time as a swagman and during the war was involved in prices investigations in Cairns. After the war Blight joined a timber firm and eventually became a part-owner of his own mill at Maryborough.

Blight's poetic career can be divided roughly into three phases. The first of these, from 1939 to 1954, resulted in two small books, *The Old Pianist* and *The Two Suns Met*. Although these contain comparatively early work, there is much in them that is outstanding and David Malouf has referred to *The Two Suns Met* as "one of the best books ever published in Australia". There is much in both which is typical of later Blight poetry. "To a Farmer, Fencing", from *The Old Pianist*, for example, is an odd meditation on connectedness and entrapment. It begins:

Where hides the spider, mortal or machine,
Whose web is stranded from each telephone?
Light bulb to light bulb strung like beads of dew?
Who is that mammoth spider who threads the dew?

I saw you fencing, where cattle were your flies
trapped in lush paddocks. You toiled spider-wise,
enmeshed young swine; and left a likely clue
— so strong a web no creature could break through.

What spinneret, freak organ or machine,
did you conceal, that eye had never seen?
You say, "A factory." Ah, that implies
some city spider trapped you with the flies.

The city spider is the banker whose network of information is the telephone system, alert to the trembling of trapped farmers.

"To a Farmer, Fencing" heralds later Blight poems in that

it uses images not in a subordinate, explanatory role where their task is to illuminate some central proposition in the poem, but as things having a rather dangerous life of their own, which are forever threatening to knock the poem from the perch of its intended direction. Blight exploits this continually to develop odd methods of attack, and a poem like "To a Farmer, Fencing" begins with a view not of the farmer and his fences but of the telephone and electrical wiring systems.

But the odd, tangential attack and metaphors that are inclined to escape imprisonment are only part of the distinctive Blight style. At some point in these first two books, Blight abandons the aim of producing a poetry which is in such control of the formal requirements of the various forms he uses that the poems will sound effortlessly smooth. It is important to remember that Blight evolved as a poet in a highly formalist period. In such an ethos, the aim is to demonstrate mastery of a set of fairly arbitrary requirements as to poem length, rhyme scheme, metre and so on by producing poems in which such features do not call attention to themselves. There is always an element of demonstration in the poems of such periods, and smoothness always seems to be one of the major goals.

Late in Blight's second book the poem "Totems" appears, which suggests that for this poet smoothness will remain out of reach, that for him "the dark/sinuous casts of a mind/sealed by eyes that are blind/to natural graces" will be the only possibility. The "clear/lyric mask of the lark" will not be attainable.

This page be cursed . . . it is the worst page
I have used as a stage
for my evocations. My poems,
like totems,
are tortured wild dreams here.

They have nothing of the clear
lyric mask of the lark;
only the dark
sinuous casts of a mind
sealed by eyes that are blind
to natural graces;

only the impossible carved faces
of wooden gods — stolid
as they are solid
and wooden and brooding;
all life, eluding.

Yet — totems.
Are they not the wild poems
of dark minds?

Though talent blinds,
still in the murk
the carvers work.

Even this comparatively straightforward apologia executes
an odd turn at the stanza break so that the totems which have
been used as a metaphor for his own poetry suddenly become
the central object and the poems become the metaphor.

This sense of a style which will not demonstrate mastery by
smoothness, and the courage to affirm that this is not a result
of less talent but instead is a result of a different vision, in-
forms Blight's next two books of sea sonnets. *A Beachcomber's
Diary* (1963) and *My Beachcombing Days* (1968) each contain
ninety sonnets and are the barnacle-covered rocks on which
Blight's wider reputation was established. They have been
widely praised for their concentration on the minute objects
of the sea, the shore and the littoral.

In a sense their subject matter offers a kind of mimetic ex-
cuse for the "sinuous", sometimes awkward style foreshad-
owed in the earlier books, for what could itself be more
awkward in shape than a fat sailor or a shag with its "sly
periscope"? Although this is sometimes the case — a poem
like "Toado" perfectly captures the self-important way this
fish moves — I think that generally this is not the case. For a
start, as Malouf notes, the subject of the poem is always more
likely to be the poet's self bursting through, preventing the
poems being objective, *chosiste* exercises. Secondly, the for-
mal requirements in these sonnets are, for a start, often mag-
nified beyond conventional requirements, especially by the

appearance of internal rhyme. There is also a tendency to pose greater problems of technique than a sonnet strictly requires by choosing singularly awkward words like "yellow", "housed", "listening", or "toado" to bear the weight of rhyme.

What is happening in Blight's poetry is a very complex and intriguing phenomenon. If I read it correctly, unnecessarily baroque formal requirements are being posed not for a chance to surmount them and produce something in which it is not obvious that they even exist, but so that their mastery will be impossible. Out of the failure of language to match form will come a new voice, awkward, not at all like prose or speech, but not like any other voice either. I think there are precedents for this: the American poet Louis Zukofsky wrote a book in which the sound of the English words would match the sound of the Latin of Catullus, and in his A— he has passages which do something similar with Hebrew as well as Latin texts. We needn't debate whether or not there is some mystical bond between word and sense which justifies this. We can treat it simply as a formal requirement (that is, that a meaningful English sentence can be made to sound like a given Latin one), which may be absurd but is not different in kind to the requirement that end words of lines should share vowels and consonants in particular patterns.

We can see something similar occurring in the highly formal patterns of medieval Norse poetry where the bizarre requirements of the *drottkvaett* stanza — something like sixteen of the forty-eight syllables were bound to each other by various prescribed kinds of rhyme, for example — meant that any sort of naturalness was out of the question, even for the most talented of poets. As a result a kind of poet-speak emerged, ludicrously unnatural but also highly elevated in tone and full of possibilities. Nothing as extreme as this occurs in middle-period Blight, but there are enough remarkable passages to suggest that something of this sort is occurring. How else would we explain the manner of lines like:

> Here you may wish
> to see a stone move, too; but the cobbles under the sea

stare patently — dead pupils. Oh, roll this cobble
to life, even such lowly life, till it swims like a bubble . . .
    ("Stonefish and Starfish")

or:

                    and I was
impressed by his rotundity. All the
profundity of the East was wound up
in his gross obesity. Yes he was cook — cup
and saucer and soup did it. See
the Globe, see the sauce on the Poles, pot
belly of the Equator?
    ("The Rotund Sailor")

The most perceptive early appreciation of Blight was by Judith Wright. In the last chapter of her *Preoccupations in Australian Poetry* (1965) she devotes some space to a comparison of the poetry of Webb and Blight, seeing them both as poets who have chosen a solitary path. Like others she stressed the originality of Blight's work, seeing him as one who "works far from other literary influences in fierce and self-involved independence". She sees the poetic process involved in the sonnets to be a wrestling with primal units of the world. Each individual crab or rock does not involve the universal; what Blight needs is a continual focus on different individual items to build up a knowledge of the universe and the place in it of human beings and their capacities for thought and creativity. Her explanation for the distinctive style is that it results from a "knotted awkward struggle with meanings and with the intractable shapes and events of the outer world".

From the perspective of the 1990s what strikes the person rereading these books of sonnets is the problem of closure. Although Blight has a whole series of varied techniques to bring the poems to a conclusion, sometimes they resolve themselves by stepping outside the complex world of the poem to a simple summarising statement. The much anthologised "Death of a Whale", for all its virtues, especially the superb lugubriousness of the middle section, at the end pops its head out of the world of poetry into the world of journalistic observation when it concludes:

— Sorry we are, too, when a child dies;
but at the immolation of a race who cries?

If we are inclined to judge poems with such conclusions as inferior because of their reliance on what is really an extra-poetic feature to provide closure, it is worth bearing in mind first that we are likely to make the same noises of dissatisfaction at some of the sonnets of Shakespeare whose sonnet form encourages three quatrains of variation followed by a couplet of neat conclusion, and that contemporary reviewers of Blight's work tended to praise such neatly concluded poems as superior to ones we might find more interestingly ragged-edged.

A poem such as "Ghost Crabs" is an example of the kind of sophisticated closure of which Blight is capable:

Ghost crabs, their fleetness, have made me
desperate to delineate the norm
of the effacing creatures. I must
describe nothing less ephemeral than dust;
and you who read must barely hope to see
a creature, an image, but a mere scrabble of form.
It is on these sticks of letters, like the legs
of ghost crabs scurrying across a page
— rustling vellum sounds, on a dry beach —
that your eyes must follow and teach
themselves the trick of seeing the cage
of limbs, the bedouin band which drags
behind horses of sand the eyes on a pole:
the only Christian sign betraying a soul.

The rhyme scheme of this poem is unusual, being made up of two six-line sections followed by a couplet. The result is a kind of inverse Petrarchan form with a sestet preceding an octet. The sestet sets up two themes and images: firstly the invisibility of the crab is a spur to description — it is a creature whose description will consist of signs of its appearance, like the description of a hole. Secondly the crab will be used as an allegorical image of writing so that to read the poem is analogus to discerning the outline of the crab. But the poem is not content to exploit these two images and disorients any simplicity by concluding with a third: the limbs of the crab become not only the shape of letters, they transmute mysteriously to a band of infidel horsemen on the sand. The image remains relevant because it uses the idea of a sign and a signifier, but the movement from the sands of the Eastern Australian coast to the sands of the Middle East, from crabs to souls, is a striking one.

A Beachcomber's Diary and My Beachcombing Days do not mark the end of Blight's exploration of this form and this subject matter. Sonnets appeared in the books of Blight's later phase and nearly twenty years after My Beachcombing Days, Blight published a collection called Holiday Sea Sonnets. Although these sonnets extend the tradition of the sea sonnets there are substantial differences which reflect and thus may be used to encapsulate some of the changes which occurred in Blight's work as it entered its third phase in the early 1970s.

One thing that occurs in this phase is that the focus suddenly widens to embrace a larger, public world. This is not to accept the inaccurate impression that the sea sonnets are about objects of the sea. They are clearly about the interrelatedness of items of existence and are thus about the human race as much as about the creatures of the sea. Questions of evolution occur regularly for evolution is one of the relationships that can be determined between lower and higher life. But the concerns of Holiday Sea Sonnets are demonstrably wider in a number of ways. There is, for example, a set of eighteen sonnets devoted to Korea, originating from a visit there in 1979. The first of these, "Poem for Asia", sets out to measure the change:

> I have never written a poem for Asia.
> That indicates how insular poems
> may be. I have written many more poems
> than a thousand, but never a poem for Asia.
> Once I made mention of that Continent's

vast shoulders and its penis, India,
dripping islands into an ocean; but thought
of Asia as a body not measured by roads,
without a sky over tens of thousands of
towns — just land filling Earth as spoil.
Placed there, the black hole of geography
into which knowledge lapses contritely,
crushed into one word, Asia. I have never
written a poem for Asia; now ponder how to.

The altering of perspective to focus on the largest of conti-
nents requires a quite different approach. If the ocean pro-
vides a whole set of complex particulars, it is necessary for the
poet to remind himself that something as vast as Asia is also a
particular, even if of gigantic size, and should never be used as
a vague single term.

This shift is not untypical of the poetry of Blight's third
phase. Retirement in the mid-1970s produced a freedom to
write and a freedom to satisfy the desire to look at the public
world. The output of poems in this period is enormous and is
only sampled in the three books *Hart* (1975), *Pageantry for a
Lost Empire* (1977) and *The New City Poems* (1980). Some idea
of the larger corpus can be gained from seeing Blight's collec-
tion in the Fryer Library at the University of Queensland.
Blight in this period really becomes a quite different poet. The
change of focus outwards generates a hunger for experience
at all levels as well as a desire to bring experiences as diverse
as love and political life closer to the surface of the poems.

Many of the images of a poem like "For Francesca" are fa-
miliar, especially the black on white which is also a metaphor
for words on the page, as it was in "Ghost Crabs". But there is
something about tone which suggests release and an even
more intense engagement with experience than the intense
observations of the sea:

Francesca! now in the early hours
when death is the natural animal,
and my skin seems black as yours, I light
my lamp, the pale leprosy $c_i$ whose glow
disturbs my after-midnight sleep;

stretching a ghostly white arm
reaching for my pen to write of you.

At the same time as this shift in focus outwards, there is a complementary shift to a perception of the poet's own life, from a perspective of slight distance. Blight sees himself more and more as an ageing man, and there are many poems like "Last Years" (If you have provender/and a sound donkey, don't fear to/travel those final leagues of age) or "The Actor" (I hadn't expected to be/cast in the role of an old/man walking city streets so soon"). The development simultaneously in these two directions is important because each buttresses the other. Comments on issues such as Australia's tendency to idolise the merchants which bleed it do not work if stated from a generalised position, whereas poems on the experience of age become pointless if the poet has no other focus but on himself. The material of Blight's last three books is, consequently, richly interactive.

Although in this later verse the same formalist perspective is evident (the poems are inclined to be written in lines of eight syllables and exhibit the same immensely varied internal structures as the sonnets), what is happening is a break from formalism. In being free to write a good deal, in having the authority to write on all subjects and the honesty to write openly about himself without the mask of self-aggrandisement or the subtler mask of self-denigration, Blight has effected a most radical break from the ethos of formalism. His poems are no longer discrete, excreted objects with pretences to formal beauty, but reflections of life as it is lived, of life as a process. In this his later poetry is close to actually enacting the insights of his earlier meditations on the objects of the sea and the continuous, growing interactions between all living things.

Martin Duwell

**Note:** The poems in the final section of this selection, "Uncollected and Later Poems", were first published in journals including *LiNQ*, *The Border Issue* and *Poetry Australia*.

# The Old Pianist
## — 1945 —

To Beverley and Robyn

# Canefields

These green ribbons will not tell you all; but listen —
The tan men weeping sweat, swearing at the town
That tears their hearts for wealth . . . the canefields glisten,
And their green sea of ribbons clears your frown.

There was a wayfarer, one season past,
Who never mastered his farewell to her,
The brown decanter of his costly mirth
Filled by each northern summer to the last.
He toiled, and in the hearsay of her bold green fur
They called the priest and pegged his claim on earth.

The canefields were his destiny. Remember?
The fan-tan thrived, the houses of your loves and next's,
From August to each sweltering December;
And still he stayed on numerous pretexts.

Yet scentless, flowerless green ribbons . . . How —
How did they bind his wayward heart, or find
More constant each green summer his deep lust?
The tan men earning for their lovers know
More than the warm earth tells; and green ribbons bind
The secret of his toil, sealed in the red-hued dust.

# The Parrots

They were peculiar preachers, wise-spoken birds
who recognised our poetry of words.
In bird store, zoo cage, or in specimen case
they saucily stared you out of countenance;
left ornithologists to put in place
their tribes; impressed you with their strange romance.

They proved for you there were such places as the Aztecs
parrot-feathered, once inhabited. Scarlet necks,
leaf-caped, with helmets beaked, arrow swift and fierce.
One winked an eye and you perceived a new
exposure of your ignorance, assumed mind's tierce
then thrust at each your finger, preening through

a sulphur-crested cockatoo's proud crest; heard speak
a 'king' . . . a 'greenie' bit your finger — stoic jest!
how the blood clot matched the lorikeet's red beak.
The macaws (galaxies of pets) 'blue-mountain's' chest
of royal hue . . . the pink galah . . . rosella . . . why?
You wondered if life fixed their dye

flying through a bright rainbow. So quaint, bizarre,
the parrots fought and filled the air like leaves
of jungle sheen, then fluttered down to dare
another look. Though nothing gaudy long deceives;
and, having watched the parrots, people wondered
whether the Artist triumphed, or, in them, blundered.

# The Hurricane Lantern

She might have been the bush pub's slattern,
but in the darkness men and women,
being alone, each had in common
a leaning towards the hurricane lantern.

On nights she danced with lambent flame,
in a shawl of lace, her flying-ant mantle.
Then no man lived could tame and handle
this bush pub slattern, the hurricane dame.

Those times she shone and vied with carbide,
or flimsy-mantled mistress gas-light;
or, bravely, when newfangled flash-lights
of some car failed, she took a car ride.

Game cigarette lighter, she, too, smoked
in her blackest moods. With her pungent smut
she filled the room till, putting her out,
the barman swore and the customers choked.

Undoubtedly, she was the gamest,
roughest, toughest flame of all.
In milking sheds I knew her well
— a trifle dull, but stout and honest.

She cast her constant light on men;
and I think that most of them had a slant on
were admirers of the hurricane lantern
and they cherish those hours she lit them then.

# It

It is outside and cannot come
into this mind without these words;
though listening be wearisome,
it cannot enter without words.
Gently at first — it cannot burst
the scarlet shutters of this brain.
The eardrums it must rumble first;
stand at the eyes' blue windowpane.
And when at length it sees a light
shining within the intellect
it then may stand, as shadow might,
outside the entrance, tall, erect;
awaiting there in dread and fear
that she within may turn no key
unwilling yet to see or hear
unravelling of this mystery . . .
Then, meaningless, may traipse and pass
across the garden plot, the grass;
and, standing at the gate, may be
for ever afterwards a tree.

# The Old Pianist

I listened, for old time's sake, but — old frame
and flame extinguished, famished for old fame,
and chill bone fingers hardened as lead comb,
and glassy heart and ear as hollow tomb . . .

I kissed, dry-lipped, as wind on dewless grass,
the dull dead greying streamers of her hair;
but burdened soul this mind might never pass,
this rib-white gate now fastened with old care.

In perished cities of young days it grew,
this grey dust of her keys; so old eyes weep,
preferring it, as gold, and heed anew
new value in her song's loud ban on sleep,

open wide windows and lie awake like day,
pressing the dark with eyeballs white as fear,
in silence hear her old piano play
day in and day out and immortal year.

I listen, for old time's sake, but — old frame
and flame extinguished, famished for old fame,
and chill bone fingers hardened as lead comb,
and glassy heart and ear as hollow tomb . . .

# To a Farmer, Fencing

Where hides the spider, mortal or machine,
whose web is stranded from each telephone?
Light bulb to light bulb strung like beads of dew?
Who is that mammoth spider who threads the dew?

I saw you fencing, where cattle were your flies
trapped in lush paddocks. You toiled spider-wise,
enmeshed young swine; and left a likely clue
— so strong a web no creature could break through.

What spinneret, freak organ or machine,
did you conceal, that eye had never seen?
You say, 'A factory.' Ah, that implies
some city spider trapped you with the flies.

Indeed, I noticed you ensnared inside
the web that's spun about the countryside;
and though the lure of lissom gossamer
will trap the best of flies, a wily spider

lurks out of sight of web upon a thread
that links a telephone beside his bed.
He sets his net and seldom after toils,
but sleeps and smiles and feasts upon the spoils.

And, knowing now that spider wasn't you,
the miles and miles of wire a maze pursue,
let's follow, find that spider spinning wire
and draw so much of it his legs will tire.

# The Song

Softly the song speaks, stranger from the shadow
and beckons me and night outside my window.
It lays its lips against my startled breath
and calls me from the void of dream and death.

Mind leads tonight where lights have shone no conquest
of darker paths the lonely heart knows longest;
and endless nights and I have dreamed too long,
and you came too, to learn this hateful song.

Somewhere our singer sits, a hidden sitter,
and sips the music till its sweet is bitter;
and, saddened, he has known himself a fool
stirring so soullessly night's stagnant pool.

The night is black, and the blind houses lonely
as though burnt-out is life. All substance only
a shadow proves to be. We spurn night's sleep
fearing a hideous vigil we must keep

lest day will never wake. So, in the shadow,
we sit together waiting for the morrow
and till that hour of daybreak must belong,
our animal obedience to song.

The song steals back. The heart's slow drum, alone,
late reveller, writhes in a cage of bone.
The vacant ear fails like a gemless eye
and dawn returns our slumbers aimlessly.

# To a Crow

You've made inquiries at the gate,
not passed inside, asked someone there
behind the grille of Death's bared ribs
— is it the heart gives secrets, squibs
of rumoured sickness? Is it Fate
garbed in a dark gown, standing there?
You ought to know, you old black crow!
Frost is a shroud as white as snow
and under it the grass won't grow;
though it covers the dead, their feet still show;
and you're not here, but you're thinking now
to dress for a hearse the brindle cow.

What undertaker can conceal
in cash demands for burial
the cawings of a hateful crow?
You're here, so let the whole world know
in cawings how a crow must feel
taking the fees for burial.
You ought to know, you old black crow,
how sick things feel when their hearts beat slow;
when others watch, how tired they grow
of Life and what it has to show . . .
But — duty! Yes, I must allow
It's duty, so I leave you now;

and friendlier in the years to come,
I'll ride this way a quieter horse
some summer's day, when ants run fast
unhampered on the tracks ungrassed;
when at a paddock shrine will some
stroke hungry jaws, hold lean discourse . . .

How sweet a beast was the brindle cow,
and how they miss her music now.
They'll talk, because her skull will show,
her spinal column in its row,
how white the bones as tombstones grow
— grim ad. to the trade of an old black crow.

# Night in the Park

White moths at the park gate mantling a pale street light
gammon — am I lonely? White picket fences grin;
for who is my soul's bedmate, but this dark night
on the dewy grass spreading its wet death-skin?

At grey dawn I shall cough, as the sun comes up.
At cock's crow I shall corkscrew from my leaf-cold bed,
bowed to the grasses my cold hatless head,
while night's worn rags expose me and the world sums up:

human wrecks are lonely, have inhuman hearts,
pick up their packs and traipse their roads alone,
leaving behind them nothing tabbed their own.
Tree-roofs above them and discarded parts

in each grey paddock. In their long years, dreaded
mind alone has journeyed, and heart despairing
stayed back with the young days to a pale dream wedded,
and each grey crinkled brain is lost to caring.

So, at the park gate, moths and a pale street light
gammon — am I lonely? White picket fences grin;
for who is my soul's bedmate, but this dark night
on the dewy grass spreading its wet death-skin?

# The Bell

I could not bend this mind, this skull-cold mind on mine
towering in wordless speech the chiming
     steep paved skies;
so lived this voice unharmed in turrets of sick ease,
tolling the dawn each day and herding at night all men.

Called down the centuries this ancient beldam tongue,
this simple heresy, sang out this brazen bell;
and culled my soul of men, that eyes may drink their fill
mocking this misery — old years to me belong.

Old years the bell had heard; now telling the ears of men
how time would take its toll and reap each hair and head.
All men had loved, but I, the babbling of this creed,
the swaying of this tongue, this gossiping beldam.

Till hope, once breathed of life, no friend would
     hear of more
and I scoffed lone outside while all prayed long for me;
till threatened by this bell, brought back this
     madness nigh,
except this voice I loved, old friendship it could mar.

I could not bend this mind, nor age infirm its will.
Rang down the centuries this ancient beldam tongue.
I could not breach that tower, tear down this
     timeless wrong;
but sang, each hour and day, the spirit of this bell.

# To a Dead Tree

How would you look in a steel-grey suit
with telephone cups for your 'pips' and a boot,
a tall jackboot of fresh black tar?
It's better you stand in the bush as you are;

not drilled on a range and holding a line
which leads to a city over the Rhine.
Who, then, would believe you were ever a tree,
or your kindred a mast in a ship at sea?

You stand here in beauty, of a forest, the bones
untrammelled by ravings of night telephones;
though stripped of your bark and your leaves, still a tree
honoured and sung of in memory

gilded by dawns that parakeets flash;
undoubtedly proud of those antlers that clash
with the moon's wide horns, entangling at night,
pricking the stars in the sky as you fight.

Yours is the battle no saint would gainsay
— to stamp in the sunshine for ever and aye.
But what if they made of your timbers a post,
how then would you stand, you gaunt grey ghost?

# Four Horses

Four horses have all day long across the plain
raced, each with a flowing mane,
through long white summer grasses, and
low clouds — wind-driven, four-in-hand
towards the sunset glow, wide nostrils red
and hooves like fire-swept foothills spread.

And I who sat to watch them pass
saw grey cloud-shadows on the grass
race as those horses might have sped
to distant passes, stallion-led,
which bore them swinging down the years
— fast meteors among the stars.

But, cautioned by the night, alone,
the Earth's grey shadow on my own
fell like the dust those horses raised,
silvered the grasses time had grazed.
It seemed Death drove behind the four;
once in the mountains, closed a door,

when all had entered, from the sun
freed and unharnessed, every one.
For, though upon that wind-swept plain
four seasons I have come again,
still watching for that team I stroll,
I have but met that waif, my soul.

# Going to Bed

I have disclosed to you one half myself
— the masked exterior, the sly self.
You have not looked under, with me at nights,
this pallid splotch of skin; seen the sights
of horrid grins in mirrors, grimaces
of demons in a hundred fleeting faces.

No — I am the Devil . . . or, I think, near enough
to frighten you, my dear. Horned and gruff
as Balboa, and I've seen as much
the other side of life. As dead to touch
as frozen carrion. Oh, cast me off!

Do not number me among your friends, but scoff
at the dying man with the greying locks
— one, with ashes, trees and rocks;
whom you may recognise only
if you be very lonely
and tired, and troubled; and, too,
see in your mirror, his bedtime zoo.

# The Two Suns Met
# — 1954 —

To Madeline D'Arcy-Irvine

# Becalmed

Above and below the ship . . . deep . . . blue:
no cloud . . . no island . . . and which of two
suns was celestial . . . submarine?
Each sailor shrugged. Who'd ever been
South of the Line . . . who knew . . . who knew?

There loomed a vessel in the sky
— towering above, or below the eye?
If thick brown kelp were drifting past:
seaweed, or cloud to foul a mast.
Why should each ship becalmed thus lie?

Below and above each, seeming sea
like a great eye which dreamily
sees nothing and by nothing is seen:
a waking which may, may not have been.
'What man of us is you, is me?'

Everything double under the sun;
and I am troubled to prove which sun
lies under which, which sun above.
'Lord, if a counterpart would move!'
but movement there, or here, is none.

'Silver's a man age cures with cunning.
Monkey, he shapes, on the taffrail running.
Agile he props, then dives right in.
Face rises to meet face with a grin.
Head strikes head with a smack that's stunning.

'No more Silver, he's under the sea,
or up in the sky — or where is he?
Lost in the ether, South of the Line.'
The eight bells rang, but we heard nine
. . . and where are we . . . and where are we?

Lord, it is dark. The two suns met
in a blaze of flame I shan't forget
. . . and which ate which, we dared not say;
but night fell fast and at close of day
we cheered: 'All's not proved double yet!'

Too soon, too soon . . . the moon that rose
danced off in twain, like silver shoes.
One waltzed the sky, one waltzed the sea,
but which waltzed which was strange to me,
for South of the Line who knows . . . who knows?

'This is the nether world,' I said.
'Since Egypt, here they've buried the dead;
under the Earth and South of the Line.'
The eight bells rang and we heard nine.
'Are we the kin whom the mermaids wed?'

Doomed on a ship that is dead, becalmed:
in a winding sheet of blue, embalmed.
'Friend, it is doubly strange, I feel,
no one will credit our plight was real:
we dead, in a ship that was dead, becalmed.'

# The Cat-o'-Nine-Tails

Given the cat, it was not only that he ran
a gauntlet of whips. One could bear that
before the mast in a salt gale, but a man
could not rally at those words — 'Convict rat!'

The delirious cat striking with its nine
tails, vigour and abandon of nine lives;
mauling him — 'Convict rat!' How refine
punishment with humour, better with knives?

Cheap gibe — the cat. It sprang again . . . again;
and pain filled in the hollows between ribs.
'Give him the cat!' said voices in his brain;
'Convict rat! we'll break his blasted nibs.'

'Cat . . . cat . . . Give him the cat!' He remembered
sentence and pretence of humour, grim;
and, when he felt through torture one, dismembered,
down from the triangle they bundled him.

What niceties of morning between bars
matched his red scars; what sun's salve
mended his hide? Better if scimitars
descended to quarter or halve

his striped agony — striped like a cat.
Such humour would intrude. He rallied now
. . . 'Milady's kitten?' How he grinned at that:
grimaces that would make one wonder how

solace approached, as near the kitten came.
'It would have done this deed — remember that!
Convict rat. It would have struck the same.'
He fondled, with steeled heart, milady's cat.

# The Turnip

Once weeding, when I pulled a skull
out of the earth — or might have done;
though looking down, a turnip spied —
I laughed. What man has ever cried
at killing plants? I mused how dull
a skull would seem to anyone
who'd cultivated as his own
a turnip such as I had grown.

To pull a skull with locks as mad
as turnip tops . . . The grim chance chilled
me. Yet, upon whose roof I gardened,
remembering, the image hardened.
If Mephistopheles once had
some semblance of the truth fulfilled,
some heads now buried in a row
would, like my fattened turnips, grow.

Would then, I mused, my fingers grope
to pull some friend's head? For I knew
the turnips claimed my friendship, too.
Weeks on their welfare I would spend
and they, fulfilling every hope,
would, at my pleasure, meet their end;
one with my enemies, the ants.
But who has qualms at killing plants?

In true perspective then I saw
a turnip face-down on the earth,
its wild locks matted since its birth;
a physiognomy so weak
— no forehead and no lower jaw.
There never was a soul so meek.
I dragged it by a lock of hair,
and for its fate I took no care.

# Sea Madness

The rocks' black sheep grazing beside the sea
in eternal green pastures which at certain seasons
are snowed with the white daisy foam;
the sheep-dog headland relieving me
of the need to watch rocks grazing . . . are reasons
for one more glimpse of the sea — then, to go home.

For I was born never to live by the sea
but to sail in a rumbling dray through brown paddocks, tossed
on the crest of a ridge — or a petrified wave.
And a voyage with stars in the rigging of a tree,
racing before a gust of sunset, then lost
in the night's sargasso, for me would have
more spirit of adventure than to sail an island of palms
through immobile seas. For, beyond the harbours of stars,
on a moonless night, I have known
vast loneliness in the West; and there my qualms,
detached as air, put off no bobbing spars
from shipwrecks, loosed to rescue me. But from the blood alone
I grasped that line, that memory of old moorings,
that magpie call from the past, which draws me back
out of deepest despair, out of darkness, into desire again.
And, if I have hated the sea, and even abhorring
its incessant story, have struggled to paint it black
with its dumb rocks, its verdigris plain,
it is because of a calling, a longing in me,
and a faith that walks the land, as One, the sea.

# Bride Ship

Alone I walk again the harbour shore
for one more glimpse of a ship like a wedding-cake
rising out of the waters and sure to make
lips slaver, but from the thought it would berth once more.

A bride ship, packed like a galley, full of wives:
laughter in place of curses and bosoms heaving
not from the lash of whips, but make-believing
that princes were waiting ashore to ransom lives

from hell-cold England. Birkenhead and space
— such places now forgotten and, instead,
matchless the white illusion of a feather bed
safe from incestuous fathers; and a friendly face,

like the sun's known only this winter . . . rooming
together in this peacock weather. The wonder
of all that distance packed in a blow like thunder
at the sight of the wharf and the start of a dream looming.

How went the song? The brothel's frenzy in this!
and plenty of husbands willing — a waiting-list
for would-be wives to ponder, let alone resist
the age-long ache of the voyage for a kiss.

No — it was not that matter of relations
who thought this other would prove the better catch.
Difficult here to dissemble, shrink down the hatch
and stow away the heart immune to passions.

The blood flowed swift to rescue the burgeoning heart;
and, the cold winters over, lust came to obscure
ghosts of that other image — too frail to endure
in a tearful dream, to hinder a bolder start.

Better the blood boiled over for none were disgraced
— except that the flesh was punished. So once they danced
under this dazzling sun and nobody glanced
at the ship like a wedding-cake, so white, so chaste.

# Crow

Perhaps blown over by a hellish wind
(charred wings, burnt bill) you have good cause to caw.
Some bushfire, first, attracted you offshore;
when, silver gull, you wheeled landward to find
those ruddy sails you'd sighted once before:
the Spaniard's or the Flying Dutchman's, east,
bringing new savours to your fish-filled maw.

But this, instead of the expected feast:
Hell's fires, red winds, infernos vast, you saw
as though the Spaniard raked you fore and aft
with a black broadside. Haven then you sought.
Perhaps, at your misfortunes, some bird laughed
— some feathered Sinbad; when, once overwrought
with countering desert spindrift, wraiths of smoke,
you changed to crow and matched the inland folk.

# The Dying Spider

A spider in his galleries of web
(as Quasimodo through Our Lady's window)
squints at each fly; limbs weaving to and fro
(swinging in bell towers) red claws that stab
at the trapped shadows. Dusk — and he has spun
many small suns that every morning
shone with a brilliance of silk; and every one
at evening no longer adorning
the marble balustrades, looped like wire
lustreless and leaden, gathered the gloom.

Often he rang the sculptured scrolls of bloom
with bell-ropes of fine thread — his belly-fire
forging a silver tenuous as time;
that held madonnas, as frail moths,
and gargoyle beetles trembling at each chime.

But to his nostrils now a thousand broths
that bathed the bones of many insect saints
steam with a vengeance. Sickening, he faints
and falls, it seems to him, ten thousand feet,
full of repugnance now for life and meat.

# Black Lace

Behind the black lace of the printed page
did you see everlasting life, or age
dressed in its leper's skin of crinkled paper?
Look! Who walks through the sheet, with a lit taper?
Who burns the page so that your eyes are red
when you have scanned its text, gone late to bed?

Yes — it is flesh behind the print's black lace,
if you can recognise the mantled face
that, peering back into your wondering eyes,
knows thoughts that troubled you; was just as wise
and just as foolish and as mystified.

In books some lingered, though their bodies died;
some, ageing, mannered, speaking to a few;
some spirit only, deathless, ever new.

The veil was never lifted, but the lace
showed well enough the presence of a face;
or, hanging on a peg, an empty skull,
it looked like cobweb spiderless and dull.

# Colour

What need to paint a world for this keen man
who, blind now, knows its oceans in such words
as: Soundings — Leagues and Leagues — and Seagulls?
And, who says, 'We came ashore that summer.
For a year we yawed through snapping ice
and I grew blind.' Who saw the ice and said,
'The mongrel pack! like yapping dogs, the floes
rose up around us, froze and locked us in,
a year — a year! and it was months too late
to save my sight. Our fated vessel, crushed,
plighted her troth in the sea's arms under.
But, then, there came a ship. They cried, "A sail!"
They cried it on the day my total blindness
set like the sun in tropic latitudes;
and, oh! their words were pricking stars of light.
In black and white they talked, eschewed the green
of seas I'd known. Perhaps they, too, were blind!
I had my answer when, at length, I smelt
hot summer sunlight blowing out of Sydney
and sensed my world — blue — gold in calm reflection.'

# The Oyster-eaters

I had heard the bird's name and searched with intent
the oyster banks, and a bird with a red bill
and a hingeing, unoiled note gave a high call
in a flat treble. Whatever the bird-voice meant,
it sounded ajar — a door protestingly forced,
a bivalve opening — shell from shell divorced.

I saw the oyster-bird with red cockade-like beak
— white, blue, red (a tricolour) plump as a chef;
and it could well prepare banquets to last a week:
oysters — *hors-d'oeuvres*. Somewhere around a cliff,
a door's answering squeak, and two birds dined together
at turn of the tide, with wind blowing us salty weather.

# Into the Ark

The clean otter, I have not seen other
than in this young man, this sailor and his brother,
the old sea-bear, potter about in the lee time
waiting on shipping to take to sea in time,
before they grapple together and, between them,
the white ghost of their seafaring is forgotten;
knifed, in a shore-ditch for a bawd who's rotten
with some disease the elder can't shake off.

Before they come to this, there's mateship. Break off
the ties of the brothel. Let them lumber the wharf
for a sea-bound vessel and be seen aboard,
again living lives that limber them for their Lord.

It's lucky and good for the young man, this land's cloud
is behind them. Like a giant stain, it has cleared
from their blue sky, the sea — a heaven revered
by its worshippers, the sailors, in the Ark stowed;
fortunately, without a dove in their ship, and faint hope
of landfall or leaf beyond the last cape.

# Monsoon

I said, 'Can't take much more!' but the rain heard,
only the rain answered, answering with more rain.
That had the sea's extravagance — depths, distances;
and glances at the 'glass' told more — our chances
zero for a clearance. I could gain
half a knot by shutting up. A word
would shake the laden cloud branches, it seemed.
Cram on more pounds of steam and thank the Lord,
no windjammers this season! So, on we steamed;
were lost to you, God, in the curtain-folds
of that monsoon, the voyage. And the holds
filled up and we grew fins. Enough, we thought,
to dry out like smoked mackerel in some port.

# Sea Brawl

The land rises and the waves rise and the rocks' knuckles
batter the tides. In the melee of surf and sound,
of shattering glass as each big wave like a window buckles
and splinters, we are as onlookers spellbound.
Such damage outside taprooms should mean war.
Such large-scale tugging at nerves should frighten us;
but there's no lustier fight than sea versus shore.
Here is a brawl to watch, with the sun to enlighten us.

See the pandanus lean down the cliff? You have seen
such ladies with parasols high in the bleachers score
wildly on some mute's cranium — screw-pines that have been
watching such fisticuffs lifelong, six decades or more.
Roll your eyes now, out to sea: a hat flies in there . . .
a sea bird drops into the waves. There is the glint
of something that shines like silver — coins you would swear.
And this is no walkover bout that a patron might stint.

Parry and thrust of the rocks, pounding of surf . . .
There is much damage here, and skying of towels.
Roar of the sea . . . of the crowd . . . deep guttural laugh,
loud hisses and aspirates wandering awry from vowels.
Here's a big fellow in blue dives into the fuss . . .
High-pitched note of a sea bird, or whistle that shrills?
Why should such turbulence hold excitement for us?
We onlookers are such fierce, incontinent devils.

# Thunderbolt

When I have heard nothing and seen nothing
after a day perishing in the grey bush
with my gun and my dog, is it proving
existence matters or not that makes me push
tobacco into the bowl and, impersonal, watch
the tortured char of a match?

That captured feeling of eyes under the tons
of ashes (our skies) and top-heavy clouds of noon
crashing in five-o'clock storms like guns
around me, oppresses. Will escape come soon?
Not out of moonlight have the arid paddocks been cut
and it is anger of fists batters the roof of my hut.

Drowsing, I pass into legend out of this day.
This way Thunderbolt rode: no different now.
The weatherboard hut that he passed along the way
is the same with its rusting tank in tow.
The slow round-up of years has altered little
but what the storms and the winds laboriously whittle.

But time is still, time. Past time and present touch
alone at the instant. Now, and are parted. Much
of doing is what is done — as when Thunderbolt
storming the instant would inflict his will
with fist and pistol, wings of a stolen colt,
while ours outslept the moment of time's evil.

# Totems

This page be cursed . . . it is the worst page
I have used as a stage
for my evocations. My poems,
like totems,
are tortured wild dreams here.

They have nothing of the clear
lyric mask of the lark;
only the dark
sinuous casts of a mind
sealed by eyes that are blind
to natural graces;
only the impossible carved faces
of wooden gods — stolid
as they are solid
and wooden and brooding;
all life, eluding.

Yet — totems.
Are they not the wild poems
of dark minds?

Though talent blinds,
still in the murk
the carvers work.

# The Friar Bird

Bracken, sand and bush . . . barely a dozen thoughts
Creation scattered here. Oh, who thinks like this?
How wizened is his mind! Thicker than these nuts'
rinds is his skull. He can't hear the hiss
of the mating snakes, where his danger lies
which, as his mind is blank, may too seal his eyes.

Here lives this world's mystic, knows its hidden smile
of the clean sands under unrevealing bush,
thigh-deep seas of bracken, sameness of each mile.
Who would heed the friar bird in the bottlebrush?
Who would ambush silence with such raucous clatter?
It is safer then for him to hear some other chatter.

But who can speak to lonely bush, who can speak with trees?
Only the friar bird may call, speak like this.
Blady-grass would cut the throats, put dead men at ease
when their tongues from talking grew black like his.
But the bush is listening still — it is worth while.
Here lives this world's mystic, knows its hidden smile.

# Camp Fever

Camped by a creek and didn't speak for a week;
the continual bell of the smaller frogs, the croak
of bullfrogs in the bulrushes, and the chirp
of crickets in my bunk. He'd harp and harp
that fellow, on the weather until, I tell you
I, maddened, could but threaten, 'Very well, you —'
and then we two fell out, fell on each other
and bitterly fought as brother fights with brother.

A bloody mess, the tent, and out he went
— his two lights out. Fell in the river. Meant
to bathe his wounds; wound up instead
as posted missing in the flood. Poor dead
cow, now I miss him. Now I tramp the river.
How I'd nurse him to drag him out and shiver
listening to his talk of weather — never
again to quarrel, or pitch in peril of camp fever.

# I Had a Dog

I had a dog limped in my shadow
Saturdays, before me — on Mondays, after,
And each understood the mood of the other, glad though
to bark, or to growl. Our sort of laughter
was never that loudness that leaps to a rafter,
hangs there too long like an echo far madder
than sane dog, sane man, chooses to hear
under a bridge where they've done for an adder
and frightened the swallows away for a year.

Camped there dark comes, darkened by rain
and, overhead, thunder — Pantagruel train.
Drips bomb, ashes fizz, ant-lions flip dust.

If I guffawed loudly, imagine — disgust!
He'd slink off, that dog, and leave me, at last.

# A Beachcomber's Diary
# — 1963 —

To Douglas Stewart

# The Rocks

It is the sea, and not this snarl of rocks, that is angry.
Just look at the sea and down at the dog-stolid rocks
at bay, fangs bared. It is the sea that is hungry,
leaping up at these others that do not know what licks
their loins to a hunger-frenzy . . . soup-bones aboil
which they are, standing in the sea. If they
should bite as in a storm, they seethe with madness, toil
as in biting a flea; sea dwindling away,
and they are exposed, show whiter their fangs for dread
of something they cannot bite. It is always
they are afraid; and, like a mad dog, mad.
Dogs, and afraid! Seems sea's like their master's whip.
Let them but sight a mast — to canine eyes
this is a limb, a leg — beware, the ship!

# The Wave

The wave is something, yet — nothing.
A green sloughing of water
on shore; is death after living.
What was it that 'Now' is 'After',
and we must look out again
for another wave? Plain — plain
that the sea will return, filled
with the green importance of growth,
swell with another wave. I shall see, too, its slough,
filmy, almost invisible — think that the snake is killed,
while the serpent's escaping in the secret grass . . .

Look down at the wet beach. All there is now
is this wet slough to step round. This we may pass;
but the ocean slides inshore — recoiling, repeats its blow.

# The Island

The island is lost ground; an acre or two
in the realms of the sea. Is country
once loved of mother earth. Now, a whale's back
of wet mud, black, sliding back out of view
into the lost regions of a trackless sea;
and far, and farther away, as the tide's slack
takes up, is submerged, or part submerged
like a whale sounding in the shelving sea
— or could it be less noticed than a whale,
it is so small an island? Even the clouds have urged,
whipped it with rain, like spray, to go back to the sea;
crawl out the primeval monster, swishing a tail . . .
There are such pleasures as becoming noticed, coming under
    the eye
of the lordly sun: an island becoming an 'I'.


# Cormorants

The sea has it this way: if you see
cormorants, they are the pattern for the eye.
In the sky, on the rocks, in the water — shags!
To think of them every way: I see them, oily rags
flung starboard from some tramp and washed
onto rocks, flung up by the waves, squashed
into sock-shapes with the foot up; sooty birds
wearing white, but not foam-white; swearing, not words,
but blaspheming with swastika-gesture, wing-hinge to nose:
ugly grotesqueries, all in a shag's pose.
And beautifully ugly for their being shags,
not partly swans. When the eye searches for rags,
it does not seek muslin, white satin; nor,
for its purpose, does the sea adorn shags more.

# Mangrove

I saw its periscope in the tide;
its torpedo-seed seeking the soft side
of the island, the grey mud-bank.
And, where it touched, it seemed the land sank
with its trees exploding from water; the green
mangroves' fountainhead of leaves bursting, seen
like a mushroom-top of detritus and spray.
Today, in my boat, at the close end of the bay,
I saw its dark devastations; islet and spit
sunk in the flat high tide. Where these war-seeds hit,
gaps of horizon and sea; then trees . . . gaps . . . trees
. . . like men on a flushed foredeck. No ease:
the drab olive-green swarming everywhere;
troops of the mangroves, uniform, everywhere.

# The Jellyfish

In lewd imitation of woman, heavy upon the tide,
like breasts upon her bosom, jellyfish ride.
I have watched them from the jetty; blue,
paler than the sea, almost a purer blue
where they drift in the lee-shore water in a pattern
that is pretty as the open breasts of some downtown slattern.
I do nothing but watch; no fishing
with the jellyfish thick in the current, fleshing
the sea with their lascivious numbers, rubbing
a line left in. Better one took to clubbing,
like the boy on the beach, knocking them out of the sea
above the line of high water, than watching with me.
I can only see these woman-shaped fish
protruding under the clear silk surface, know that the sea is rich.

# Porpoises

Porpoises, so far from their green, salt garden;
led up this river-path by a lack of rain.
It is strange to learn that the sea is so close.
In their snort and dive there is depth
such as I never dreamt the river held.
So narrowly between these banks I see
the ocean's menagerie pass. It wakes,
astounds the eye, twenty miles from the sea.
Watching, processional, the porpoises cavorting upstream,
they seem so like young horses: horses, I know,
that bow their necks and speed without stress.
Drought must coax them to come here again,
to give the river new thought; even though, I fear,
they'll be gone for the season's cycle, like any circus train.


# Small Fry

I saw such tiny fish: they'd take a year
to swim a dish. And they were swimming — where?
Their journey did not there and then appear
to matter; but I have thought since, and share
amazement — not with them, I'm sure. Going,
they were coming to that very point, I'll swear,
where river and sea meet: a balanced flowing
in and out, a tide of chances. Washed up, washed in;
never could arrive at a destination before death,
unless by waterspout. Sucked up, splashed in
some country town, with fragments of rare
hail and rain which take the cowhand's breath . . .
who'd gasp, 'Fancy it raining fish!' and say,
'Isn't it the Father's gift, and Friday?'

# Stonefish and Starfish

These are the first shapes: stonefish and starfish.
Imagine the stone falling, tumbling down the scree
through a rarer atmosphere. Here you may wish
to see a stone move, too; but such cobbles under the sea
stare patently — dead pupils. Oh, roll this cobble
to life, even such lowly life, till it swims like a bubble . . .
I looked, longing, too, into the lonely deeps
but knew I watched ages after the first star.
If I could will life there, raise it by steps
to perfection, would it be as we are?
Starfish, I know you, now, staring as I have,
where a star would long gaze for its image to move . . .
These are the first shapes, life in its first steps.
See, now, man gazes into the outer deeps.

# Death of a Whale

When the mouse died, there was a sort of pity:
the tiny, delicate creature made for grief.
Yesterday, instead, the dead whale on the reef
drew an excited multitude to the jetty.
How must a whale die to wring a tear?
Lugubrious death of a whale: the big
feast for the gulls and sharks; the tug
of the tide simulating life still there,
until the air, polluted, swings this way
like a door ajar from a slaughterhouse.
Pooh! pooh! spare us, give us the death of a mouse
by its tiny hole; not this in our lovely bay.
— Sorry we are, too, when a child dies;
but at the immolation of a race who cries?

# Beacon

This man in the blue-striped guernsey, this semaphore,
just why he plays, he does not know. Half-back
in the tide, little less than a mile off shore,
on the sand flats, where tubby boats tack
the slack channels, sidestep his post and slats.
He's hard as knuckles, can take a good blow;
tackle of tides won't pull him down. What's
in his football make-up makes him slow
to come ashore with driftwood, stuck,
as he is, in the bay mud? Only a boat's tackle,
a kick from its keel, in the storm's ruck,
would send him off field; would buckle
his straight, hard knees; break up the line
of beacons that stand like footballers astern.


# Crab

Shellfish and octopus and all the insane
thinking of the undersea to us is lost;
at most is food, in our higher plane.
But what of this submarine ghost-
life, without its meddling monkey? Can
the crab regenerate into prototype merman?
Sea, of nightmare pressure and mask-
green faces in the gloom — what is your task
in creation, or is it over? Has space
such a tragedy of planets trapped? Was
Eden thus? Oh, pressures which the lace-
sponge of the brain survives! What has
the life of the sea of my ignorance
but such creatures; much of this wild-shaped chance?

# Garfish

Creatures that live in a wave, glass-housed,
luxury-living garfish, yellow-lipped
and pretty as flat-women. Slim-hipped,
bubble-sipping surface-livers, espoused
by the sun. Garfish that are not fish
but meteors, in the eyes of the star-gazer
— star-dripping meteors that the dozer
on the mud bottom would trap in a wish.
Sinker-sodden star-gazer, sick and sorry fish:
while the flappers are storeys up — gars
in the planetarium drinking bubbling spas;
off-this-planet plankton, trifling, for a dish;
and catching a breaker now and then —
it, a late tram crammed with white-shirted men.


# Cone Shell

The shell lives cleaner, more delicate for me,
although I know it's dead — the poet shell!
I wished its creature no harm, but knew well
it could mean death, alive: a bee-
sting magnified to lethal dose. Close
to the sea I found it, where I trod
gingerly in the coral. God,
if he made it, made it, I suppose,
for me to find it thus: polished a little
by the rub of the tide, and hollow . . . hollow.
Remembering the creature's work — the fellow,
himself, no doubt (no doubt!) not worth my spittle
— I gathered it, and have it in my fine collection
of poets' works: a shell of pink, of near perfection

# Carl

Snails build mansions of pearl, but my ex-earl
— for such he must have been to love leisure so —
builds in the snow of the sand-dunes a low
tin shanty; windowless to block the wind's swirl.
Old Carl, for such is the name of my ex-earl,
loves light though, combing it on the beach.
And what does he do in the dark shanty for speech,
but listen to the tin flapping; his old girl,
the sea, talking, walking upbeach with the tide.
When the stars are wide awake watching Carl
in his old tin shanty at night, one pearl
he guards, one pearl he has found — his pride
and his strength — that mystic, moon-crazed sleep
which he in his age struggles and lives silently here to keep.


# A Dog to Tie Up

If the sea must beat my door, hungry animal,
poor dog with its tail, rapping a tin with its tail
for two meals a day, two bites at the beach,
remember, it has no words to frame its speech;
but speaks cunningly nevertheless.
I am at no loss its meanings to guess;
and to understand the great fawning beast
is to possess more than land — a guest.
And who has a guest at his door has
all wisdom for his learning; has
the sea, as he says, 'sighing, or storming'; has
another's problems to exclude his own; has
the ocean at his door to deal with; has
a dog to tie up each tide — his dinghy; has . . .

# The Anchor

Know then, the only joy of an anchor — to be strong,
have iron arms, and be long
immersed holding by cable a ship
like an iron kite in the blue, deep
waters of a port. Know then, the anguish
of its cross — to lie as stone, while fish
hover and flutter like leaves, and love
bites, in a barnacle, a red groove
into its flukes. To be the 'pick'
in common talk, thrown over through slick
to the dirty bottom with bottles and tins;
an anchor in all its servitude, its sins
flaking off in rust like a scurvy:
yet straining to hold a city in heaven — cause topsy-turvy.


# Erosion

The beach I knew is a splash of the sea,
whiskered still with brambles, wanting
the blade of the breaker to shave it clean;
like clean sand, colour of flesh, and free
of all this turbulent foam. Taunting
me as the process of shaving. Mean
mirror that fragments shows: the rock — the nose;
the reef — the teeth; mouth hard — as the blow-hole blows.
Let it go under; let the land sink. Let
the land be shaven again. I will stick
out no hand to arrest tide in its sweep.
Lather it briskly, thoroughly wet;
let it be shaven by the razor-wave's lick;
whiskers and brambles succumb in its soap.

# Rope

He had a long arm, the sailor had;
a yellow-scaled arm that uncoiled like a snake
and, in the green water, slid down to the rock
and held the ship still, as though it were dead.
Like a goose, in its coils, it fastened the ship;
and, though the winds blew, the ship never sailed
— the goose never flew; the grip never failed . . .

he had a long arm, the sailor — rope:
rope that knew only the strength of the sea,
and matched, with its fibres, each fresh blue tide,
current and swirl, with its stay and guide;
and danced, then a jig, as a 'hand' toil-free . . .
with a roll and a swing — and a blackbirder's blow
on any bare back, at feet that were slow.

# Place of the Tube Worms

Where the cathedral-pipes of the tube worms on the rocks
bare at the low spring tide, I gather a fancy of churches
old and lichen-encrusted. In lonely searches
of these Sunday places, where the tide mocks
Sabbath cycles of worship, I come in my search
inwards, as outwardly, it seems, looking for crustaceans,
molluscs, brown seaweeds — and, finding them, what
      each means.

It is asking for living's reason, makes this seem church;
and, not unlikely, the mosaic of the tube worms' casts
surmounted by the barnacles. Still at a lower level
the brown gloom of the seaweeds hints of the devil
devising graves in these catacombs of the tide; as some
      fiend blasts,
comes at me with a crash of columns and light
— comber from the unknown — with Samson's might.

50

# The Beachcomber

I have lit upon the old man's secret, know
the error on his brow is like the error
of the fragile wave whose mirror
after mirror crashing builds yet its character. So
I know he likes the ocean beach best, will escape
only on Sundays to the lee of the cape.

It is his converse with the breakers, playing ducks
and drakes with our conventions, makes him somebody
excusable — one man like a poet: shoddy
in morals, quarrelsome; who bucks
society, and, for his sane rebuke,
is allotted the space-room of the beach;
respected there, given a friendly look
if they can nail him — sought for his fish-tall speech.


# The Headland

The hill of grass near the green sea is
wave-mocked, wind-raked; never has
crashed down on the beach. But rocks
in the surf prove, when enough clocks
have ticked, finally, the sea will come
and comb the base of the hill. Some
day — destiny decides it — holocaust
will break the long grasses' rest.
Quicker pebbles, first, skipping down
into the rising sea will drown;
then the headland will burst open
and all the sloping, silk field shapen
like a smooth green wave will have
its kinship proven to surf and a wave.

# Chinamen's Fingernails*

To have worn some distinction that, severed
from body and soul, is distinguished still as belonging
as seawood to triton, as fingernails to a Chinaman,
is some power of achievement. So I gathered
the shells, the long ones only, belonging
to Chinamen; though I could not question a Chinaman,
all seeming, here, long past dead; and just their nails
like talons of porcelain lying in sets on the beach.
And though these were true shells, what likenesses!
    what libel,
to have called them Englishmen's nails, when pigtails,
a pair of chopsticks, were not needed to teach
their discoverer their name. Even on Babel
they would have had their portrayal, the same in all speech
spoken, had a beachcomber peddled them there from
    this far beach.

* Common name for a species of shellfish, an elongated bivalve found on
  Queensland beaches

# Sargassum

The wild berries of this seaweed are like
bubbles; the khaki berries that break
with a snap undertoe, like bubbles of
sunburn. I would look for doubles of
our pepperina-trees in a drowned village,
seeking the sea plant from which the waves pillage
the little sprigs of sargassum. For I know
the hot country where they sing, with a slow
summer's drone of cicadas, our pepperinas; and these
little floats — not berries — seem like those trees'
adornment: 'mid fish-spine leaves, once red and green berries,
in the foliage of the trees. And I realise
it is also in the rainless, blue country that we
find the pepperina, like sargassum in its own desert sea.

# The Sawfish

Isn't it ominous that Nature has not yet cleared
away the carpenter models of her evolution?
So the sawfish still threshes in the shoals, and should be feared
as the first pattern of a saw. When chaos
rules, after the last bomb, the solution
of the bomb's rebuilding will be there. It would pay us
to catch all sawfish, first. What a haul
of sea-things will be necessary, not to leave us a trace
of hand-tools. God, what a slaughter and burning!
Even the hammerhead shark with its maul;
the swordfish with his sword — not a trace
of such patterns must we leave — or, learning
from such prototypes as auger-shells, pipe-fish, at fish-schools,
we shall build up the terror again, for our remnant of fools.


# Spring Tide

After the spring tide is the very low slack;
a long drawing back of water. All that
seemed harbour-like is a mudflat, black
with its wet mud, and its drowned cat.
Oh, come in, spring tide — low-water is known
— though ocean is disappointing to the middle-aged.
Such years want a tidal wave. Too much is known
and unknown. The trivial thought is staged.
It's the unreal, then, is real: giant waves
washing over mountains . . . incongruous detail
out of tubs of ale. Mind craves
that which only the heart may have; knows it must fail.
Oh, come in, spring tide! high-water is known
and the heart's slack, below which love must drown.

# Bluebottles

In the warm currents, the physalia sails
— Portuguese men-o'-war, the bluebottles.
Flotillas of the physalia, in floating poop-castles;
each like a vessel of the Armada, armed with flails,
bombardier, cables of torture and fire.
Oh, unwary swimmer naked on the rack
of the wave, feeling those whips on your back
— do you not fear the sea, gasp in the mire,
grope from the sea's noisome moat; lucky to escape
contorted, deformed by pain? While children dance,
caper along the sands at this wild sea-chance
that throws the physalia up, foundered beyond hope
of ever seeing Portugal, or Spain, or Europe,
or the Pope, or whatever Power lies beyond the last cape.


# The Cotton-tree

It's . . . it's that old man of the sea, again;
shaved on the beach this morning. Curse his beard,
fouling the surf, tickling the girls' knees. Feared
by the gulls. See — he's flushed them! Plain
their scatter, wheeling over the dunes. Strong,
too, an iodine smell where his blade
bit — the seaweed tossed up like whiskers, long
and tangled and dank. What beauty has made
him undress his weird face, like the moon,
now Tonga is widowed, Polynesia diseased?
So peaceful the sea looks and pleased,
like love come lately; while over the dune
I see her, now, the wild cotton-tree; never far
from the beach, ever a flower in her hair.

# Periwinkles

I am not against living again, like these
which I watch; perambulating rock pools,
climbing near death in sea anemones;
with their thatch-roofed cottages, or shells
— periwinkles. All the base sludge I leave,
the snail-slime of my workaday, I trace
to a seashore cottage, and a grave
by the rocks protected, in a lonely place
where sly gossip enters only like a creeping tide;
and I shut my door to more boisterous storm . . .
as I imagine periwinkles to have fireside
comfort in their shells and be warm,
though the sea is cold, and the immense
world, outside, an unfriendly fence.

# Sea Beasts

The sea horse, of course, can't canter; the sea hare
never runs anywhere; while the sea cucumber
isn't a vegetable at all — but fable says
that men of China eat it for dinner, and there,
in China, along with sharks' fins and birds'-nests, number
it among delicacies; though it's a sea slug, no less!
All this topsyturvydom of the sea proves,
through such nomenclature, man moves
in a looking-glass world . . . all that he sees,
dreamed from the lees of some experience he suffers,
toping the heady bottle of the world's globe.
I do not think, if the seas were ink, these
records could be closed, with all that offers
as double proof his sea beasts need some scientist's probe.

# Ghost Crabs

*for Miss Lenore Smith*

Ghost crabs, their fleetness, have made me
desperate to delineate the norm
of the effacing creatures. I must
describe nothing less ephemeral than dust;
and you who read must barely hope to see
a creature, an image, but a mere scrabble of form.
It is on these sticks of letters, like the legs
of ghost crabs scurrying across a page
— rustling vellum sounds, on a dry beach —
that your eyes must follow and teach
themselves the trick of seeing the cage
of limbs, the bedouin band which drags
behind horses of sand the eyes on a pole:
the only Christian sign betraying a soul.


# Ocean

Great Powers are only good for themselves.
Tell me the ocean cares about my cottage
clinging to the seashore until yesterday;
now, undermined, leaning on one of those shelves
that the high tide and wind leave. I'm in my dotage
if I think Providence ordered it this way.

Just that great, greedy sea, eating, and biting
more than it can eat immediately.
The stately headland will go, along
with the snarling reef. Ten waiting whiting
will shuffle in silver slippers; and, greatly
bloated by the tide, the sea will poke its tongue
out, over the land, satisfied to barely wet
a salt-pan for which, a foot above sea-level, it would fret.

# Rocks and a Ship

All about us there are envious rocks.
Why our ship moves, while they're stuck stock-fast,
seems to confound them — so many solid blocks
of space abandoned to an archaic past.
If there were veins of metal in them, some gleam
in their dross, they would not be such a dead loss.
They have to be buoyed, marked by a lighthouse beam,
because in their steadfastness they are dangerous.
If you run on them — consult them, as it were —
you will learn how obdurate a point is
in a straight line. Steer around. Don't defer.
Give them no second look for a near miss.
The wonder is not in them, but in the sweep
of this shifting ground, the moving ship.


# Old Winds

The wind from its station in the south
blows constantly — the south-east Trades.
But, stubbornly, propeller-blades
slog the tramp-schedule wrong-end-about:
North, or south, a port with freight,
no matter if the Trade Wind's late.

A wind has blown its purpose out,
as oil is 'in' and sail is 'out'.
And God's convenience of winds
ends with a curse in skippers' minds
who slog the Trades wrong-end-about,
when cargoes call not north, but south;
not west, but east. Even old winds
end with their casualties among old friends.

# Meridians
*to Jack McKinney*

For whole centuries there may be tracts
of ocean never approached, only
netted by meridians. In these lonely
vastnesses such netting protects
them from disintegration into space.
They were, and are, will always be some place
in the ocean where a ship might pass
or a plane plummet, and may be found
entangled in the net. As the years pass,
some time we'll find in the net a rock, a fragment of ground
thrust out of the sea by submarine volcano.
It is the net will hold it in its place:
the net we've cast around — a flimsy lace
to hold five continents; yet, strong enough.


# A Sailor's Grave

Shall I be buried at sea, or shall my bones wait
till the continents float apart, and at the gate
of my grave I hear the waves grinding
the granite back to sand, and feel the blinding,
stinging salt in the voids where my eyes were once?
I, wearing that white cap, my skull, a dunce,
should read the portents of each feasting tide;
should watch the ravenous currents devour the sand;
and I shall learn high up on a mountainside
is no safe place for a grave. What part of land
that has not been the sea bed? Then out to sea
bury me with all sailors, and I shall have
feel of that permanence that befits a grave
with, ever, the wind and wave to moan over me.

# Sea Urchins

Scraggy heads, sea urchins — black enough
back of the ears. Mates in a pool. I suppose,
smoking; else, why those black stubs protruding?
'Spines,' you say? 'Spines for movement!' Tough
on an urchin's feet, walking on spines. Those
egregious urchins, unlike their brother sea star duding
it as some Yankee sheriff's outsize badge,
have won more sympathy, begun more smiles,
beggaring their way on the sea bed, walking miles,
like marram grass ranging the dunes at the sea's edge.
Rolling, tumbling creatures. How express
their natures better than name them sea urchins? Feckless
wandering ugliness; yet without that brute
preponderance which makes land's larrikins seem mute.

# Speaking of Age

There are those intangible fences, higher still
than a boy's kite, or its guardian hill . . .
I speak of age — of an age when to speak
is not to be listened to, unless some freak
trick or gesture's chosen. I cozen the young
people still to hear a poet whose old tongue
swings like a bell with tower-ropes broken;
who has had his say . . .
                            But the spoken
word echoes still, and from the kite's hill
I hear 'Hurrahs!' I had forgotten when
a mere child of ten. I did not think then
there was much magic lost in the wild notes
of a boy's cries. Now, high over fence and hill that voice floats.

# Fisherman and Jetty

Old jetty, wade with me out into the sea
and there let us watch ship and shag pass;
knee-deep I, thigh-deep you. We
with our reasons to be there: standing in the glass
sea, rod in hand, crane on deck;
each under scrutiny, looking a wreck,
yet part of the scene which people on shore
come here, long hours, to gaze at . . .
'Will he catch a fish?' 'The jetty is more
like Japanese torii with that
missing wood decking.' They're speaking of us.
If we were on land, they'd never discuss
two such old derelicts. So — the sea honours all,
the quick and the dead, that age in its thrall.


# Mud

Fat, flabby, as a woman's belly — jelly-like mud!
neither land nor water, but a black, crude
substitute lying primitive and rude
in squalor and poverty: a quadroon of the blood
that the sea and the land mixed with a skeleton of wood
belonging to neither — conceived in the flood,
the blind surge, and low urge of flats that intrude
under the white sea — the worm-infested, nude
land deserted by the tide — flesh that's never had
the bones of ice to brace it; a skeleton of wood
rotting in its carcass — black, filthy mud
conceived in the crazed swirl of torrent and flood,
green slime and grey ooze seeping through its blood
— yet, stone in embryo, firming into nationhood.

# Dugong

Dugong lumbering by the big ship,
sighing suggestively till seamen think:
these might be the old fat wives
of salt-junk sailors. The hare-lip
dugong with pig-eyes that grey-blink
as they roll over, leading lady-lazy lives
of too-fat mermaids. The dugong belong
to a legend and are thought lost,
nearing extinction. Not they. The men
who hunted them, the aborigines, long
since are lost; still here the ghost
of charmed Ulysses might sail, chained, again,
as long as this were midnight, roll an eye
unseeing, fall in love at their fat sigh.


# The Landfall

There was a tide-mark on the jetty which
marked this side of ocean, and so the leagues
seemed meaningless after our landfall — pitch
and toss of the long weeks when sea-legs
ferried us, numbed us ashore. Nobody
down the long, strong jetty spoke a word.
No wave to carry us, but the shoddy
bus on the beach, and a screaming sea bird
handkerchief-white, a gesture of
departure, once over the sea wall's eyelid
closed — with the sea out of view and the stuff
of our sea trip grubby around our feet. 'Rid
of that damned, dirty weather at last!' someone said,
while names like spiders crawled all over our waiting-shed.

# From the Inland

Since these months, I have not seen the ocean, its clear
thought of flowing, the clean flash of sea,
keen, steel glint of saltwater, dear
is the memory. I cannot be
fond of this landscape of hard shapes,
the never-ending change of matter. Give
me a paddock of surf, where daisies drape
wave-crest and trough, though such blossoms live
in impressions only of white foam and gold suns
— the countless golden suns, the white daisy-foam,
where the greensward of ocean runs
up to a beach shanty some sailor calls home.
Here, in this continent's inland, this shed is a shed.
Where there is no dream, all fondness is dead.


# At Sea

Place and object are unknown here — where?
When I was a sailor, I was told at sea,
'See the golden sunset, in the sea and air!'
and I looked, and all was gold to me.
Then there came a blue day, and a grey;
and, 'All the world is colour,' I would say,
'but place or object, there is nothing there
— air is air, and water, just like air.'
When I was at sea, I knew so little care,
for I met nobody, and was not anywhere.
But the sea was blue, and the sea was gold,
and sometimes red, and silver. Old
and young alike all knew: 'Out there'
was no place or object but colour, water, air.

# Gull

Gull over the ocean, hung on unseen wires,
life's Chinese kite to frighten loneliness
— so, my soul hovers. It is as brave, tires
only when life's day ends. Then who will guess
its roosting-place, wonder whether on wave
or dune-crest with the restless wind
that troubles sea and sand ceaselessly
it struggles? Wave, as thought after thought in the mind;
all repetitions of hours, days, years, find
it no wing-span nearing knowing. Wave after wave
— the endless ocean of gull, of mind;
for bird and spirit there is only a sea,
its loneliness to frighten away. O gull! O kite!
hover with my questing soul through death's long night.


# Iceberg

Strange range of crystal silence; living glass
gliding, glistening past us, blistering white.
Taut piano-string of sound; ear-vibrant wall;
precipice of stillness; thunderous rock-fall.
Oh, hidden knife; oh, disembowelling thrust;
hammer of great might; rock none shall pass.
Ship's soul of death, death-dealing in your night.
Woman, so beautiful whom none may trust.
This is all feeling and adventure, this
phantom island lost and found again.
No summary of its beauty, or its terror,
completes its full description. Say it is
lack of heat. Say it is Nature's error
— solid lighter than its liquid. Say, 'It is . . .'

# Dolphins

Dolphins are intelligent beings thronging the briny
in orderly numbers. According to Pliny
after viewing the holocaust at Pompeii,
when the sea receded, and in the vacant bay
all shapes of monsters lay gasping in mud,
the dolphins were there, hyacinth-hued
in death. He even remarked their colours
in a time of disaster. Such dolours
as afflicted the universe, affected them so,
in that hour of dying, they had to go
through the full range of the spectrum to show
each self, even in death, like a rainbow,
a living covenant that not alone
man lived aware, while they cruised off the main.

# Surf

When the ocean with the motions of a washing-machine
washes the green tide into the whiteness of surf,
laugh, oaf, at your indolence on the beach.
This was no invention of yours — what does it mean?
What — which one of us does it teach?
Not one that he is in paradise, oaf.
No — the wind blows and the tide flows,
where all is thought. Yes! all is thought.
It makes for the stone's throw: all invention.
All about movements of surf, some thought-device knows
— its curvatures, stresses, its tension . . .
I can't tell you. Such knowledge cannot be bought,
but thought out, somehow. Somehow it is thought out,
or the surf couldn't be there, only vacuum of doubt.

# Shells

Where find beautiful skulls, like the molluscs' shells
whose sculpture is eternal art of sea-
and lake-shore? . . . the 'arks', the 'angels' wings',
cockles and scallops. To be dead and leave
beauty, as imperishably beautiful
as the common scallop! There dwells
art in the atom; there is perfection to be
envied by mortals whose imaginings,
whose great cathedrals, I scarcely believe,
attain such achievements of art as common cockles.
You would doubt me? Have you looked over my collection
     of shells?
The red-mouth stromb, the black-mouth stromb, the
     flowery stromb?
Oh, for a Taj Mahal as glorious! Such shells
live after death, are not just Beauty's tomb.

# My Beachcombing Days
# — 1968 —

# The Rotund Sailor

A fat sailor! I met a fat sailor. I
believe he'd been cook — was very rotund;
a fat sailor, so very rotund. Try
as I have, his name I cannot remember, and
that's my particular trouble, because
search, search the world as I have, I have not
found my rotund friend; and I was
impressed by his rotundity. All the
profundity of the East was wound up
in his gross obesity. Yes, he was cook — cup
and saucer and soup did it! See
the Globe, see the sauce on the Poles, pot
belly of the Equator? All — all were his.
He could laugh. He could laugh. Now his
    laughter is all that he is.


# Typee
*after Melville*

You'll, by the look of the bay, sail away
from land on this wind and find a cay
where, concubines provided, you'll stay
until . . . until . . . 'Never,' the indians say
'Leave us.' Never leave the indians; they
have been left to destiny, know only the grey
monotone of sky, sea and a flat bay
— no Gauguin paints for them. They, they
are hospitable people with nothing to say.
Sit around all day. It has to be all day.
Against diversion sets the wind's deathray
focused on eternity. Blow, blow that way,
it will not matter; this is a stage in that journey,
a stage in monotony set against Death's longer stay.

# Sea Birds

Strange! They will not own us. No sea bird sings
our music. We call them wild. Hirelings —
tame cockatoos, our gardens' magpies, thrush
even, which patronise our birdbaths. We hush:
it is the whipbirds, catbirds, lyrebirds, mimic.
There is this one note certain — no sea bird seeks to trick;
none such will entertain us. Expect distance
to distort their early recognition. Just a glance
— they're swans, they're pelicans, they're geese,
whimbrels, seagulls, snipe. If they were police,
they'd not suspect us more. Is it for
the reason that they live along a shore,
that they have seen our fish progenitors;
in evolution deem man's 'better' is their 'worse'?


# Helmet Shell

Something martial, some bestiality of Rome,
incongruous shellfish, bestirs your home.
Such a slow mucous brain filled that dome
that I cannot think other than that some
imperial artist shaped it — helmet, or tomb?

Surely a mind is buried that wears for Rome,
or Russia, or America, or any Caesar whom
the gods make mad, such head-gear?

And, now, on display in a city shop, 'mid fear
of the Bomb, helmet shell, you appear:
dead — dead and polished like a skull. Wear
such apparel, Life, when Death is near.
This has the shape of a skull, and is a mere
skull in effect, that cannot keep out Fear.

# The Sea and Infinity

He sat by the sea, and he sighed, 'Infinity.
Ah, Infinity!' But there was another side
to the ocean — an eastern shore, a north, a south . . .
each was a limit, a boundary
to his knowledge; and the ocean, wide
as it was, was not infinite. Strange word of mouth
— Infinity. For there was the sea linked molecule
        by molecule;
and the sky, atom to atom; and space
by each wave-length of field and field; and all of nature
        the rational, natural order and rule
of space-time was finite in time or space.
And there was nothing that he could call
infinite but Nothing. And what is Nothing?
He has not seen it. It is not the sea. His own imagining.


# Voices of the Sea

Voices of the sea — its infinite forest voice,
soft interminable hush of calm. Choice
of no birdsong, but a sea bird's cry
— scream or screech we may deem it. Try
to define it. Try — try and the
very endeavour stultifies. Not sob, not sigh,
not wail, not growl, not howl . . . not this,
nor any sound performed with an epiglottis,
a voicebox. Noisy alien sea
peopled by wraiths that cannot speak to us;
only its crushing voice, or silence. Music
of a ship's bell? (little enough sweetness)
. . . unintelligible gurglings; off-beat
slough, slur . . . Echo unwilling to repeat.

# Ear Shell

It lay like an ear — it lay here on the shore;
strange like a pink right ear iridescent with charm.
The voice of the East it had heard . . . sun's roar
at sunrise, surf-shock and storm's alarm.
And pierced like a cannibal's lobe, its edge,
with neat perforations, passed through the vast surge
of rumour and shock, and captured only the valid
voices of worlds — of the waters, of the solid
rocks. And my hand shook as I picked up the shell
so shaped like my pink right ear. Clapped to a rock
by its living creature, this ear, as of Hell,
Earth's inner hammerings, torment and shock
it had heard; and, when it was dead, then, only in death:
wave's ripple, gull's call, and wind's whispering breath.


# Plankton

I have watched plankton over reefs float by
in rivers wide as seas that strained belief;
but, most, the shapes so intimate that I
could think that children drew them. Sheaf on sheaf
of comic drawings, unspoiled primitives
that couldn't live, yet represented lives
so simply limned; and, yet, seen here alive
too difficult to understand, so make-believe
and yet alive. Have you seen plankton float,
barely an outline round transparent space?
It can here represent whatever crayons trace
extravagantly wild. No nature note
has chronicled such shapes. Only a child's quick mind
has realised this life so naively designed.

# The Coral Reef

In the baroque style of coral, India,
Java, your conglomerate gods assemble.
Having just walked the reef at low water,
I have a fear of their numbers, a psychic tremble,
a mental numbness at my failure to describe
their Nirvana, their inscrutable jungle of peace
— a peace that is death in stone. As though a rib
were stolen from every mortal, each piece
cemented in place a monument to mankind — a reef?

I walked it — walked on the faces of its gods,
on their many visages . . . on my own belief,
I fear; exhausted my many moods,
my paucity of words — a failure at expression
by this mass of death; unable to follow its vast progression.


# Black

Soon, I said to my atoms, you must go back
to the no-land of unknowable black;
peer through its sea of loss at that blanketing lack
of light, at that solid void. There can you swim
in dreams, or fly, my atoms? There can your dim
beginnings remember the ungainly fish
that swam into fowl of the air, with flash
of insight into inconsolable man?
Think, as you ever think in the monotone
of oneness that is nothing, the numbness of black;
and as nothing think, and from such thinking make,
again, your mistake of man — embody shape;
because you must have shape and, with it, hope
and life; throw off death's awesome cape.

# Lakes and Seas

There is not such beauty in the octopuses
that one would laud their graces to the muses;
and, yet, the picture of the sea refuses
to seem the sea, if we exclude these molluscs.
Leave out the sea stars, cuttlefish, and these?
As well deprive an elephant of tusks
— pull down the windows and shut out the breeze!
It's all so stale, this sailing on a lake.
You cannot make a lake into a sea,
no matter if, in subterfuge, you fake
there, cuttlefishes, sea stars, 'octopi'
in plastic likenesses. For, in such places,
deep drowned, for ever, beneath the surfaces
of rain-fed lakes, never octopuses, you see the
        drowneds' blue faces.


# Queen Fish at Wolf Rock

I felt like the Devil, and the queen fish
rising to the lure of the spinner were
as angels, fallen angels. They were spirits bolder than rash;
some impure greed, some lust, thrust them towards the lure.
They were foolish, had some weakness the Rock couldn't trust;
and the Rock was their guardian. Dangerous
to all who approached, yet acting host
to the queen fish, the angels, the fallen angels.
And I that leather-browed devil who dangles
the illusion of a feast, who mangles
the perfection they all had, now come
to examine their slaughter, and do not care
because they die without prayer — dumb
fish that died, that could not shed a tear.

# From Fish to Man

I have lived life alien to that which I'd choose,
as fish live in the dark loose scuffle of tides;
I am that fugitive whom the heart hides
in the blood's red dangerous ooze.
Is there one moment yet, before I forget
in the depths of deep death to escape the net?
Small space, it seems, in momentary dreams.
Silent, grotesque, onward life swims
so, only the shoal is there, the shadowy shoal
proving the fish swims, but to what goal?
Yet I am he, the shape — man, the norm;
if once as fish, here in man's form.
Heart which has changed me to man from fish,
can you design of man his greater wish?


# The Spit

It is undersea half-tide, it is land
at low; and people walk out on it
gathering bailer shells, and helmet shells, and
all kinds of jetsam washed up on the spit.
Some day, the seers say, they'll make something out of it.
They'll dredge the channel, pump the sand,
and build it up, raise the spit
above the tide till it's all dry land;
then fill in the shoals behind the spit.
All's been blue-printed, thoroughly planned:
the cubic yards of shell and grit.
To those few fellows who beachcombed it,
and found life's solace on the spit,
it will be banned, it will be banned.

# The Point

The point is our objective. Who can stay,
sitting unexcited, in the lap of the bay,
when there is that venture of land pushed out
— a finger poked at infinity, a doubt
raised? Only the very aged can sit by the bay;
children run round the beach, the men in their boats
short-cut experience. There is no time to wait
while the point's not been reached. It may
show us what sea ever hides: islands, and
spouting whales, dolphins, great liners, land
drifting away as an isthmus. Nobody knows
what, some day, someone will find in front of his nose.
It is a point beyond which the eyes can be blind.
Let us run out to its venture, mind after tumbling mind.


# The Dead Shearwater

That was the shearwater that bundle of dull black feathers
now lacking even the lustre that black sometimes has;
a seabird spreadeagled by death. It was
defiant of death till this day. Seen in all weathers,
combing the breakers, dipping into the sea
like a living arc, an indestructible sea bird which famine
alone could bring down for us to examine,
not even to bury, now leaving it not to be.
What rafters of flight on the wind's arc,
like the lattice of steel bridges, kept it aloft?
It signalled in classic parabolas that the wind was soft
and the drop from the cliff-top was not so sheer and stark.
But there it lies now, the ruins of its flight;
no pyramid left to haunt us, but a scrap of the night.

# The Diver

Here at last the shag's sly periscope appears.
Watching that breathless bird, I harboured fears
of his non-appearance as he, diver, dived.
That was because above the sea I've lived,
know little beneath its surface. He must know
a lost treasure there, though meaner minds bestow
a mundane purpose on his porpoise act
— he's after food; is quite a pest, in fact,
so the statistics state: last year shags ate
more fish than Sydney places on the plate
in vast statistical weeks. But shags survive
and so does most of Sydney. I would dive
for every bite I'd take, if with the diver
I could swim down his turquoise submarine river.


# Toado

Shallow as the gutter where the toado
rowed his little hulk of poison body
past the mud-stuck beacon, the torpedo
of the shovel-shark stirs up the muddy
sea bed. Off goes toado. Not to be believed
the shark won't eat him. All bigger fish eat smaller fish,
knows toado, until it is perceived
our fish, alone, may consummate his wish
to be the largest fish. That's toado. Oh,
he's a bully fish — a bully fish is toado.
As ravenous as a seagull, and as eager to grab
a scrap, the meanest mockery of food. No crab
loves better hors-d'oeuvres of beach putrescence.
Here swims toado — his white teeth speak his presence.

# Pearl Perch

There are those fish that swim ever in the dim
recesses of the reef. A visit near
the surface means their swift demise. They can rise,
but never high as flying-fish that skim
across the seas, fleeing from deeper fear.

Yet I have ever marvelled at their eyes
when I have hauled a specimen aboard,
upon the deck have seen their gaze despise
our meaner air, and stigmatise our skies
by dying; seeing nothing to accord
with their deep consciousness — no Lord,
no Saviour? No Saviour! Have I, too, seen amiss
the airy vacuum of heaven where
these eyes at last leak out their dying stare?


# Ball's Pyramid

Ball's Pyramid. Ball's? Nobody's!
I'd say it was the sea's,
or the sea birds', icing it.
But nobody could sit
enthroned on this, not even Ball;
because it is an islet rising tall
as a legendary castle,
and it has not even a small
platform of rock where man could wrestle
with the Spirit which possesses it.
You can see Him spit
birds at the inquiring winds, sea birds,
sea birds like stars. But as for mortal words,
shout them that way, they will return to you like soot or grit.

# North Cape

*Oronsay* nears New Zealand, sights North Cape
— a land is easily found, once on a map.
Tipped with such antennae, it takes the shape
of a long caterpillar eating a green leaf
of the Pacific; and, perhaps, some quaint belief
among its inhabitants, makes this fancy seem
part of their legend and no idle dream
of mine; for, later, in Palmerston, and
other places, I had noticed cottagers had grand
bright butterflies of giant size nailed
on their house-fronts. If I have come here, failed
to study their legends, forgive my ignorance.
North Cape so cropped of timber, at a glance,
speaks caterpillars, forgetting their romance.


# The Breakwater

This sea water within our breakwater
makes a harbour for quiet reflections. Hewn rocks
here rival a reef's rocks; especially when mortar
of limpets and the sea's moss confirm
their fixture. Although, like a child's fallen blocks,
this sea-wall of cubes can form
impediment to storm. It becomes loved
as a toy, by every boy-fisherman in town.
This is just tumbledown architecture — rocks shoved
into the sea, odd and rough-hewn.
Thus were the tumbled ruins of antiquity.
But who would care if these once formed a city?
Here they conform, in disorder, to a sea plan.
With their beacon, they are now part of the sea, unmindful
          of man.

# Russell, in the Bay of Islands

I sighted parts of Russell in a game
of parallax played in its Bay of Islands
— threatening passengers, quite privately, who came
to borrow my binoculars, with stone-axe violence.
Russell escaped me; from what I saw, it seeming
immaculately white, green roofed, and dreaming
in enchantment which it always shall retain
from that hour, henceforce, unless, again,
I travel on its Bay. Then can I be
more certain of its substance. Like the pea,
under which islet hiding I would find it,
might prove a puzzle. Russell moves
round its Bay of Islands. Let him with nosegays bind it,
who cherishes a boat and islands in his loves.

# Seagulls

Gulls live athwart the land. Sea birds, I've found,
don't fan their wings like seagulls. They glide,
like the gannets, or thrash the air, like terns
which twinkle in flight like stars;
but the lazy gulls that abound
off our coasts use their wings to ride
on the back of the air. One learns,
on a sea-voyage, how lazy they are:
like kites at the stern of a vessel.
Vassals of seaports, never venturing
out beyond mast-top to the horizon.
Birds of the littoral, quite unwilling to wrestle
with high winds and seas. Praised, though, a-wing
over Sunday beaches, where word of their seeming
        seaworthiness is won.

# Shells and Skulls

Death leaves them strewn on the shore, embedded in rocks
which were once mud of the sea floor.
Yet women and children gather shells. It never shocks
them to pick up shells. Skulls? Say no more!
Shells and skulls do not seem alike
except both may be white. On a background of black
shells look like gems, while skulls, bones, strike
terror in our hearts — insignia for no Union Jack,
but the Jolly Roger, pirates' flags! Why that
distinction of grace which death strangely saves
to bestow upon shells? Shells are the outlines of life,
its graceful shape; bones, like a hateful knife,
hide in the innards, sheathed in dissembling fat.
Shells tell us of life's pride — skulls, frightfully, of its graves.


# The Sea Hare

You were not, in your own habitat, the hare.
You lumbered there
in such lugubrious slow rhythms that
I scraped you from transparent shallows where
the lesser surge was tumbling your fat
improbable sea-shape.
Oh, that I could care!
when neither that which made you, nor the gap
between sea slug and man, provided hope
of any safer progress than such chance
gyrations. For, with conscious glance
into the deep green pool, from tripod stance
— two legs, one arm — I saw a dozen sea hares,
approaching children laughing (such posture!)
    and, Who, trapped unawares?

# The Volutes

If it matters — which trees dispute — to shift our ground,
these volutes do so but, doing so, house-bound,
the sea's removalists have proved it sound
always to stay at home. Stay home yet move around!
That seems to call for sea-bed caravans;
and for a hundred million years such plans
have stood them well; and such a rigid stance
of staying at home yet taking a sly glance
at the world around them has stood them well.

If, in our opinions, we, too, could stay
within ourselves, yet learn to move away
from the one viewpoint, there might come a day,
a hundred million years hence, we could say:
Man's studies of the volutes stood him well.


# Lamprey

To see, on film, the Great Lakes invaded
by the lamprey to the stage where, unaided,
the great northern salmon faces
certain extinction, places
a complex of guilt upon Man.
Because of his ingenuity,
his clever skipping of aeons of knowledge,
he has let in the lamprey;
and, now, that rare meal of fox and bear, the salmon
in those great waters, drifts to the edge
of extinction. True! man let them in, the lamprey,
the gruesome devourers of salmon. They
attach to the fish, like Medusa's serpent locks.
Oh, how first sight of them chills one! Man needs such shocks.

# Kookaburra Shells

*for Val Vallis*

They'll show you kookaburra shells
at Gladstone, where the mollusc dwells
on sea-flats. One immediately tells
these are Australian molluscs. What else?
Now, were they found in Greece they'd be
mistaken as misshapen by the sea.
But, tell me, why a bird's shell-effigy
should so exist? And why one such as he,
the kookaburra? Giant kingfisher, may be!
but no keen fisherman, he shuns the sea.
An awkward looking shell, without the bird
its conformation would seem plain absurd.
But, kookaburra! that enchanting word,
to make a shell like this has lured the Lord.


# Fish Eagle and Prey

And so he was plucked from his kingdom by a god
more terrible than ours, talon-shod
and vaguely visible. And the blue heaven dropped
beneath them, and he felt the burden of weight
in the thin air as the eagle took flight
to the nearest rocks, and chopped
at him with its scimitar-sharp beak.

'Look! . . . See!' I said to the children; and they screamed.
'Chase him away. Get him away from it.' It seemed
I should fly at the eagle; but was strangely weak
and indifferent — a father-figure who'd failed
to save the seized mullet, and might
never again be respected, but railed
at by children, for ever chasing an eagle in flight.

# Flatworms

On rocky foreshores which picnickers avoid
in the hot weather, or shun when hard winds blow,
we know now, life is still enjoyed
under each heavy rock by the slug-like slow
flatworm, denizen of the rock-shelves of the sea.
But there are seasons he is wont to show
himself above, on surfaces of tide-exposed
decaying shale; a point I did not know
till after my first flatworm was disclosed
flowing — he moves by flowing, though it's slow
movement — over the sediment of mud
which in bay-water settles where the flow
of tides can't scour. Oozing like foul blood,
like a black tongue, wafer-thin, he roves promiscuously.


# Chinamen's Hats*

I hope that Chinamen will always wear
hats of celestial shape that I see here;
though I am looking at shells, false limpets.
We've always known these shells as Chinamen's hats.
Their shape suits almond eyes and the Orient's features
which I can't fail to associate with these creatures
and Chinamen. Chinamen's hats!
Try prise one loose from the rocks; the tong's secrets
may well lie fast inside. Though we may bash
with stones this simple cone, or wash
a loosened univalve, what will we learn?
That a myriad living beings earn
frugal but sure subsistence under such hats
which the sun and ocean would never afford to Dutch bonnets.

* *False Limpets*

# Ant, Fish and Angel

Part of me, in the morning, may be an ant
or a fish swimming away, as I spit,
or defecate, collectively fouling the bay.
So I am part of my world and can't
escape the bare truth, I am part of it;
that, somewhere, an ant, or a fish swimming away,
is a part of me. Oh, ant! oh, circling fish!
stay, and look hard at me. Is it your wish
to be part of man, to devour his innate fear?
Into the maw of an ant I disappear.
How trifling — be it a minnow's appetite
or some great fish in a more sizeable bite
disposes of me — as such to reappear!
Angels and gods come bite and take your share.


# The Finn

A seagrass chair his haven, he sits along
a low veranda where cane blinds let in
a fish-spine pattern of sunlight and a strong
smell of seaweeds — Eric, a Finn:
the old Finn fisherman who's tied up here,
a pensioner enjoying pipe and beer
and talk of ships and tides; who sometimes holds
a sextant for no purpose but to feel
his bearing's right, among bright marigolds
like suns in miniatures which his hut's keel
ploughs under; letting us know, by guess,
he sails a course of calm unhurried ease
oblivious of all signals of distress
which stem from captains tossed by sterner seas.

# The Passenger, Sorensen

The great bollard, like a grey toadstool, was
his choice of seats on deck. Because
he sat there, looking at green areas of sea,
searching where only horizons could be
different, he was a little old gnome to us.
He would not even look our way; the fuss
of passengers, even the ship's company did not
divert his gaze fixed on a point's spot
somewhere mid-ocean. So fixed, his gaze, he
might have seen albacores, a white whale, we
couldn't imagine even — which, if you stared long
at him, made you feel lonely; and suddenly strong
nostalgias functioned, making you slip back among
the crowd's consciousness, fearful of hearing a siren's song.


# A Child's Essay About the Sea

Tides come in, tides go out. There is all about us
the movement of waters, the motions of fuss.
Even the shallow ripples discuss in whispers of hush
the boat pushing into the beach. There is a rush
and surge of waters to tell you of its landfall.
The sea is never silent. The sun, the moon, and all
heavenly bodies are dancing upon it. The sea
is never still. Be it a cloud's image, or be
it a passing gull in its mirror of calm.
There, in the distance, is a tall waterspout like a palm,
or a whale spouting. Children shouting along the beach;
and dogs barking — gulls quite unable to teach
dogs that dogs can't catch gulls. A constant turmoil
of tides; disorders which the steadfastness of the land
         cannot foil.

# And About Phosphorescence

The round tank of the ocean reaches far
as the eye can see, and contains every star
and the image of the moon. They are
constantly filling it with light. Swirl an oar
and their phosphorus glows. Step ashore
and slap the wet sand, and, once more,
a repetition of stars. They have been filling the ocean
with light, all their light-years. A potion
of time and starshine the sea is. The notion
of night at sea as dismally black is a joke.
Not since Phosphorus, the morning star, first woke
has there been any cessation of light
pouring into the ocean. It is just as bright
in its fastest deeps, where fish seem alight.


# Mrs Carmody

When Mrs Carmody walked down the wide beach,
walk was an ugly word, for she could teach
the tide to flow, the sea breezes to blow
easily, gracefully, without any show
of turbulence, petulance, vicarious motion.
Oh, Mrs Carmody was as fresh as the ocean,
as pure, and as deep. I imagine, if
I fell asleep, sleepwalking over death's dark cliff,
Mrs Carmody would catch me in her fair arms.
Mrs Carmody . . . Mrs Carmody — nothing alarms
Mrs Carmody. She has one husband and one little child,
and she smiles at you with a smile that's not wild
but kindly, saying: 'I would be kind to you, too;
and all of the world with my charms I would woo.'

# Farewell to a Ship
*for Robyn*

If the earth were flat, I'd see that ship yet;
but an hour ago it was gone and I
could only stand and gaze at the sea.
And that was the loneliest parting there could be.
A plane journey — farewelling those who fly?
The mind seems quick to appreciate that the jet
can return like a magic carpet.
A car, or a train? I know as it passes by
it is tied by a road, or a ribbon of rail to me,
as if to my finger. But I cannot walk the sea.
I cannot forget that shutting of an eye
as the horizon like an eyelid shut;
losing sight of the liner at sea,
leaving the blind blue void of your going away.

# Hart
## — 1975 —

To Freda

# Home

and where? it was at some moment
I can't remember, being an old man
still loving the sight of flowers and
young girls which age parades for me:
good reason why one cannot find the house

of which there is not a trace except
the building in which he was seen younger;
where youth would enter now like an unwelcome gale
shattering the old louvres, slamming part-unhinged doors
only to lay ghosts which are not there.

no: there was never, now I find,
any place but the slow pace which on a clock's
dial he mistook for home. tell me
yet, is the same search persevering?

# For Francesca

Francesca! now in the early hours
when death is the natural animal,
and my skin seems black as yours, I light
my lamp, the pale leprosy of whose glow
disturbs my after-midnight sleep;
stretching a ghostly white arm
reaching for my pen to write of you.

Only my hand like an albino spider
sidling over the parchment traces this story
which, somewhere, midnight dictates of you.

Francesca, my totally black Mistress! I
know now, in waking there is no more
knowledge than in sleep. There is
this feeling, only, of my love for you
heightens the hour, the ceiling of my
consciousness; but beyond the lamp's glow,
up, up, all is black as the night still.

# One Night

it is one such night of the many,
indistinguishable; at home, late, only myself
. . . living? because I am the only person
awake. The house is my grave? . . . except
there are, oddly, stars visible through windows
and I can hear a wind stirring in
some never sleeping trees . . . I am at home.
Could be a millionaire . . . but I am saved that
disgrace! . . . a pusher of heroin, or a
motor mechanic? Nothing of these, but
a poet; too far gone in that calling
to deny it, to be denied. My face is
a white clock in the mirror. I couldn't
help noticing, glimpsing as I got up for a
glass of water.

# A Day

Who has seen a whole day? I thought I'd lost
one. Sunny, too. Diaphanous. Instead,
the long chore of a dull search and
nobody, nobody, helping to look because,
I see in the gloomy streets, they
are out looking also; and the weeds
and the grass have grown and they
meet each other with mowers, mowing
Sunday mornings away, in their
search.
        The street is agog with
these head-down mincing jaws; leaves
are scattering and sticks, and a
stone from a David's sling hits the
Goliath of time. One down, and they all
stop, standing around the prone body
of Mr Smith. His heart — not a stone!

All look at him, disturbed because
his face, it isn't fierce any more.
He was a surly neighbour; but he might (we fear)
have found a spare whole new bright day.

# Racialism

when the speckled hen laid a white egg and
the black hen laid a brown egg, I knew colour.
we kept fowls then, friendly fowls, and only
Sam had his head cut off by Dad and I
have abhorred poultry on my plate
in the fifty years of my own determination.
but I eat eggs, only white eggs, the
Black Orpingtons are not kept by the
poulterers, only the White Leghorns.
good policy in a white Western country in the East,
some fool judge under his periwig may determine.
nothing racial about it! the blacks were better
pot birds; but we have eaten most all . . .

the bell is ringing (they like meat) the front door.

## from The New City Series

### I   The Book

Indeed! our lives start not at a beginning.
Must you open a book that way? I lived a
different life. When I loved I was
a little older than infancy; but very,
very young, still some years in from
the frontispiece. There was a lady when
I was twelve seduced me, drew out my liver,
flayed my religious conscience. Why do
we worry then about a god and angels?
They are on Earth and of our own making.
Later, as sceptics we spec random pages.
Throw it away if the story is so dull.
Another and another paramour — that is the
tale they bend an ear to — much nakedness.

### II   Morgan

More than Morgan, I desire to eat people,
wondering in a frenzy — are there any
white-skinned cannibals remaining?

It must take place now in the very high
buildings. I have seen hawks there.
There are just bones of people, clothes picked
to rags . . . their eyes, pools of blood . . . some
in the cramped pose of old clothes thrown down
in a bundle awaiting their collection.

by the in city police at nine-o'clock
when the white cars prowl again near
the odd parks and places. It is enough
now to lift my eyes, because I see it
all again — the wild hide-out, Morgan would
have accepted.

## IV   The New Brick Building

*our family has a nice grown-ups' picture like*
*the new brick building, and you will find one*
*on the architects' board, or in the newspapers.*

the new building strangely has its tiny theatre.
we saw them drawing aside its curtains — or, one man,
*him*; with his name on a stone larger
tha the smaller uniform bricks . . .

it said *chalk* . . . or *cheese*? it was some
improbable nomenclature as names are.
who hands them out? they are hereditary
— excuses? i'll buy one, tough, like *bricks* . . .

but no! a stony silence. *for it wouldn't*
*grace foundation stones.* very dangerous if, that way,
you trifled with signatures — buildings would soon
        fall down.


## VI   First Thoughts

Oh, what a comfort! We ease down now in our
pink suite on the 52nd floor. The sky's near by.
They will not fly their planes near us. Angels,
only angels, may look in at us through windows
that have an aquarium glass fixedness,
stay closed.

            It is always winter here. But not
so cold that we can't twine a leg, an arm
together and have a warmth of soul; like a
plant's wish (here, we are plant-like). Plants!
no matter how we here took root.

                                        We hold
these rooms now, you and I together.
Let's not fiddle longer than it takes to touch;
then into, intertwine our limbs in that grotesque
embrace of fornicating vines.

                              Our prime intention.


## VII   Headlines for Anna

my toughest assignment is to remember
uncles and aunties; and now, strangely,
granite . . . and Agatha? she was my first wife
and under which stone I buried her
now that I know the *Project* is to
proceed — beginning and going ahead
rapidly! There were three wives I buried.

On a starry night I may retrieve one's bones.
But I must beware the moon — it was this, first
betrayed me.
              I may be more than silhouette
as I dig, dig, dig . . . dig up the past.

The murder was a quiet one. Why now
disturb the headlines when *Peace* is reigning
              in Vietnam?

## VIII   Neighbours

Morgan drained his eyes away from me.
I felt them run away like rivers
— dried up. Now the mountains didn't
reflect, but were wearying
barriers between nights.

                      When one doesn't
speak, neighbours are cataclysmatic — a
forbidding fence, their silence.

                             Dust
in the valleys, where the tongue lies
parched for conversation.

                         But when
Morgan spoke again . . . rains!
of course; and we stayed out in them,
childish almost to the point of
saturation. Ha! the enjoyment of
saying, for the saying's sake, little
    things.

# Evolution

Remember, while you are sleeping here, offshore
in the night, less than a suburb away, more
than a suburb of people in numbers, the fish
are awake and swimming much as they wish.
For they had their design to evolve as fish; just
as your ancestors escaped from the primal dust
to be sportive in trees, and walk on the earth.

Remember the incidence of birth
which made them fish, you man? Yet can you
take comfort from your shape as man; or do
you wake in the night with them, hear swish
and slap of a tide; knowing to have your wish
again, to evolve as angel now, you must do these things:
don sheets, wear stars in your hair, fix tinsel wings?


# Leaves

All manuscripts should be hung in the branches of trees
for leaves to speak in their many languages;
not suffer the hardship of being unintelligible
to many ears — just foreign bells
jarring out matins, or the long hours of day.

I would like to sing in willow
the true voice of China; and follow
my reply in eucalypt; and something I'd say
would translate into large-eared maple.
Imagine the many tongues of South America.

Oh, solace I don't think would sigh in conifer needles;
and the burnt trunks on battlefields, incapable
of speaking at all, would bring a
furore of silence, where deserts and cities lie treeless.

# The Letter

Better one thin frail line of friendship in a letter
lonely as a lost white glove, than never
knowing your whereabouts; in which poxed port
of travel guessing you ailed in fetter
of fever, hunger, or anguish of ever
finding your way to return. Resort
to pen and paper leaves not much more
than a pale white dream of doubt — much as I said,
your lost white glove; but in my hand
a dream of substance, form that you once wore.
It fitted your slight hand; and from it sped
like a white bird of welcome to this land
— much as I said, like a lost white glove.
I have it pressed to me, this hour, with love.


# Coober Pedy

Almost that first morning I believed
Coober Pedy was an hour's jaunt. Then
in the hot sun of noonday I knew it was
a longer journey due to our dwarfishness.

                                    Not arriving
by time of sunset, we men bedded down on brigalow
(branches stripped and layered thick as mattresses).

Chas. forgot it was another day
next morning. 'Come on, come on — get up!' A day
when we men barely spoke. It took some decades
to convince us that we didn't understand where we
        were going
— Charlie, an older man, died, still standing up.

And am I any nearer to that terminus
at Coober Pedy? I longed to journey there,
finger its opals, many years ago; forgotten now.

# The Proof

The terrible part is that while you are reading this
your life is passing away — mine, too,
which is more important. Yours is your 'biz'.

I am wondering if I am capturing, in the moment, a find
like a vein of gold that goldsmiths can use and re-use;
an element of pride that will let me remember, for a time
I lived inexorably; so, now, I can't be erased,
at least for fifty years — the lifetime of most notoriety.

Meanwhile, it doesn't matter. My name is known about
by a few hundred gentle people who bought my last book.

They look at me askance, for it is poetry
— or is it? This is the small wonder; and this
is my business, now, to convince them, my only chance
of making a proof stick longer than a scrap of newsprint
        survives.

# Statue in Flesh

If they weren't there, those unmistakable
dugs, would I bother to look twice, and
at her face, once? For that is a
flattering ratio — and, having seen the
Gorgon, I know which part of me has
turned to stone and I am proud of it,
living long after Adam and the shock
of his shame.
                    Yes! I'd say these first
seduced my itching palms; and where
hands lead me there is action: grasping,
fondling, groping and finding a way.

Why! there is a valley slants down and
I'd expect a well there to tongue and
wet my lips; and — whoever passed and
never cast stones in it, if not to
plumb its depths, to ripple, or foul up?

Don't tell me I am standing only as sculpture,
Felicia. You have a woman's flesh and
exposed under your locks, your shock
of snakes' nest hair, your nakedness is
enough to perform for me all of the
Gorgons' seductions. Lie prone. I shall
            cast stones.

# Barbara

My greetings to Barbara in the far interior
at a sightless grey point on the map which is somewhere
satyrs and prophets inhabit. I stop,
or the going onwards will overstep
into oblivion. The skies are steep
there, the waters lie deep, there is a hill
has a road up which never leads down.

Now, in those wastes, spread the rumour, I shall return.
She will stare into my photograph thinking,
not of the commonplace, but of mentors
who never existed, but taught in the purer sands
of Arabia where there is nothing but sheiks and camels,
and even the dromedaries' dung
lies uncensored, unretched on by flies.

# Night of the Full Moon

She was bright, vibrant when the clear veranda
framed her as the unforgettable full moon.
Standing on a balcony, so free from
my cramped view of Earth, what else was She?
I knew about svelte mantraps. I sought her for
that O of worship, without preaching:
learning how to, not to, love — a lesson
of time spent in holiness, unfragmented by
brute words; thus, the wonder. Just time spent
on a veranda at full moonrise; I, there,
music without listening, soothing without
hands.
        I fixed my eyes on her like a white
woman's breast; as men agape when they, too,
glimpse that unexpected nakedness. It made night
much a boudoir, and my fancy bringing in
from the veranda one bride moon for me to
sleep with all that night, enjoying absence
of all rivalries.
                Come out again, a
month's time! Will there be no fog or rain,
or will all access close? Because full moons
each last all night, while days are piecemeal;
none such soft as night so peaceful on
my white veranda when the moon shines.

# Hart

About this time, Hart would not listen and
I shouted. That was my undoing. Command
was in his hands. The people near me stood
around. They weren't leaving — yet, I could
gauge their departure from me. Age, old age!
Usage of an old pot, cracked. Montage
of my past use did not impress them. The
instance of my anger brought upon me,
from the margins of the crowd, ridicule;
while those in the immediacy stood cool
and unperturbed at my rash presence. I
thought: water when it drowns you must comply
with attitudes like theirs; no spine for your
support, an all-surrounding eye, no shore
where beacons may instruct you. Drown alone
as every drowning creature has, stone
man! You have been looked on by the Gorgon's eye.

But it is not enough to drown, to die.
Your presence is required yet, in the crowd.
You are used still, a plug, not yet allowed
to spring the vortex, Death. Old men must stay
awhile to buoy the spirit of some man of clay,
some current sculpture of success. For their
deaths, yes! old men's deaths, agitate some scare.

'What? Did the old man die? A heart attack?
Stand back . . .' but not the waters drawing back
for Moses; just to let the dead breathe, not
contaminate with death the meeting spot.
'Remember — Hart! old Jack, your partner, dropped
dead here last year.'

                'Remember? Yes, it stopped
the business for a day. Cost thousands. Years
I carried Jack; a long time. Bought his shares.
Set his widow up . . . What's your poison?'

                               No, there's

no concern. A watery substance like
a club bar crowd will never roar or strike.
The tide backs up each morning, some time;
and, p.m., there is the evening rhyme.

# The Iron Bedstead

In remembrance of my parents? Rare to
me, still somewhat beyond sight, I'd pray to view
an iron bedstead, wrapped in rust, in earth
again (as my dead parents) or still cycling birth
and death? Impersonal, except to me,
that nuptial couch structuring the
obscene, the sleep, the dream of many a
tired whore.

        On it my shade was born, and the
fresh roses of my mother's nipples meant
gardens flowering at my birth; and where I went
thereafter, always there a rosebed. I
could never think it otherwise. To try
to desecrate that garden would take much.
Not even though I murdered would shame touch
its peace, where I'd return if paradise
were certain.

        Dreaming where the bedstead is,
I never saw it. Strange! I never saw it:
and yet I dwelt on it. As surely, It,
as here on Earth: which makes me wonder, if
I dream of life as sculpture, fondling you.

You are some other token. I forget
what cannot be forgotten. Could there yet
be sparks of memory would glow from infancy,
it's then that I may glimpse the wonder of
a universe; my contrapuntal world of
lust and not-enough resolved, the doubt
of this adulthood I am living out
turned back towards the infant still in me,
the rosebed that I crave — or fail to see
that iron bedstead ever and opt out.

# Kafka's Dream

the wrong door opens and in goes
foot. Not what I expected, or
desired; but in goes foot and
hands reach out; not that I wanted
touch. Senses which I was really
not directing — eyes looked and
tongue testified.

      I dwell, in mind, next-door and
haven't entered, but they have
nailed my name (not that name
I would have chosen) above a
door, so that everybody can
see that I, in person, know
the caretaker.

                   They don't know where
I store my cherished bed, and yet
they bruise with stones and looks
(imaginary stones — indeed!)
and know the long passages of the
slander along which I must falter
breathless to escape with no breath
to explain, to ask — where is an
exit?

      I am not told: I am a shadow,
not knowing even self, or
those other selves. Each can be
silent, or the magister of noises, or
the footsteps of the executioner
creaking on the  staircase.

A hand that touches my thin
face from a dark corner is a
slap. Self judges self, without
a final verdict.
I can't withdraw my
foot. I stand part inside, agonisingly
waiting, watching.

# Eye

The trouble with my neighbour, speaks
an eye, is I can't watch him; not unless
I take a mirror and stare at
self: ourselves.

What bears comparison when
we compete, in company, but a lowering of
eyebrows — not a pleasant look.

Close one
eye, we have a wink and one must play the
fool. I always loathe a winking fellow.

One doesn't know the act behind the
curtain of an eyelid. Does it screen rehearsal
of my part as dupe? One eye is
sore, in trouble, from the stone that's cast as
dust in little gritty sentences of spite? You
can't be certain of a wink.

Later, in
doubt, both eyelids shut. That night, the
snoring soars between us;

and, next morning,
both eyes open, switch from left to right.

Only if each holds some
lover's eyes with mesmeric stare, can
one convey more soulfully, meaning
of such obtuse angled glances.

# Living in Our Town

Our Town is a draughtboard of streets. Slow game, here,
too, when you watch the moves. Child, in Our Park,
I sat watching old men playing on a
large cement replica. Each held a rod
and shifted a 'man', slowly, as Death
takes each Old Family in Our Town; with
its house, like a square, staying vacant
a haunted period and, perhaps, never filled;
blacks and whites living apart, more like 'men'
taken at each end of a board;
the streets of Our Town running straight out
into the heat haze of old tins and anthills.
Music is a balm mixed on black and white
keys at Miss Blank's, turns time grey here.

# Wind-up

When I went on the staff picnic with
Joan in my car chiding, and I
crashed in the comforting way
that won't kill one, but conundrums
the way one will live with one arm
and one eye missing, without means
of support visible, the vision
of doctors and nurses, after, became
through one eye compatible with
needles and potions which, poured
on a grub, would kill it and make it turn red
like a crab cooked, or a dilly of prawns;
then one had chess for a likeness of living
and chances of bright sunny days were *verboten*.

# Town Drunk

I end up drinking rain on the
hardwood steps; lucky they're
two of 'em, not one more to bruise me.

But drunks get no stiff necks; always
sleep this way. Never get hurt
on the boards — it's the day's

hard cleaning up! 'Hoi! Kicking up
again, Bradley?' . . . old sergeant's
soft. Runs me in for shelter,

makes me wash'n feed. Old
country town bush-whacker john;
not a copper, 'im, like those tough city screws.

Got a chance 'ere. Don't know where
it comes, but there's beer somehow.
Even Ugly Dulcie slums, takes off

me knickers, washes the ol' man;
has to sober me to get it, but
she does and I can . . . but the

week's work! Off I goes again.
Doesn't change, the bush pub,
Ugly Dulcie's pub. 'Out — out with the dogs,

Bradley!' Got to sleep again on
the hardwood steps. Stumbles, the cat, will
come purring in the dawn hour; knows

me. I'm stiff Stumbles ain't me woman.
'Pussy, pussy, Puss!' . . . bit of splutter, but
Stumbles knows me, teeth out all over with ants.

# Down from the Country

When we came down from the country, we were strangers to
      the sea.
The rise and fall of waters without rain,
the lunglike breathing of the estuary
caused our amazement; and the white stain
of salt on the rocks, when the tide receded,
where we were used to dark mud that a flood leaves behind,
held us enthralled; and we needed
some mental adjustment which people noticed. When the mind
is confronted by such magnitudes of sight and sound
there is no mask for refuge in frown or grimace;
but the face looks blank, as if it were dragged up, drowned.

How much loneliness is there in a different place,
out of one's shell, out of all knowledge, to be caught
out of the dullness of self by such alien thought?


# Palm-trees

Palm-trees in the marshes, on the beaches;
I see them, also, down the river's reaches.
Palm-trees where it's hot, to fan the faces
of the poorer multi-coloured races
— even to feed and house them. Kindly palm-trees!

Only our wars, like hurricanes, to harm these
ambassadors of peace. To mow them down
must make the gods on Mount Olympus frown.

O fabulous Palmyra, graced by women,
you would have been a weary wayfarer's heaven.
As to a beachcomber, now, the sight of green
palm-trees is paradise enough, seen
on his trek . . . with milk of coconut,
a woven mat for bed, a palm-leaf hut.

# Castaway

Man on an island, who doesn't remember the
clock's calendar; has no mirror except
a calm lagoon, so transparent he
looks through its mirror at subsistence,
continuously stalking a more vital need.

How can he, unless one day is a
stingray's barb, jog memory or
believe it's another day, nameless?

His forgotten tongue should not frame words or
bruise the air with maniacal laughter.

                         Allow it
doesn't, the sane silent man is one true
entity. Birth was . . . death . . . each is an
end. Bones bleached to lure crazed seagulls
to coraline white beaches. They ensure a
swagger.

# 'His Best Poems Are About the Sea'

*Penguin Book of Australian Verse*

It finished their writing when we dirtied the surf
like the lace of a harlot's panties; besides which
I am too old to advantage myself of its beauty
which I find now synthetic with the purchase
of sand for its far-famed beaches, at approximately
a dollar a grain . . . and those kids constantly
riding the surf — the surfies off the headlands
where the great grey-nurses paraded and even
seasonal whales.
          All now has the beauty
and flatness of my neighbour's swimming pool
which is blue.
          Blue, pure and beautiful!
Blue skies of the tourist brochure. I am beginning
to loathe that colour with its aura of beauty contests:
seeing the winners, knowing their fuck is not far away.

# Flinders Map

Flinders' waters, these. I combed our beach
off which he'd sailed its leagues. I like to speak
of leagues and kindred knots; such speech
sounds nautical, has atmosphere I seek
speaking of Flinders. Like the Admiralty Charts
you buy from Harbours & Marine, which show
His soundings, His authority. Navigation starts
with Flinders in our Seas. What more we know
is mere embellishment of Flinders' soundings
— a channel silted here, new sand-banks there;
but basically the same. The sea-lane's windings
as Flinders mapped them painstakingly, with care:
6 fathoms, 5 fathoms, 4 fathoms — the numbers only, printed;
by dint of seamanship no soundings stinted.

# Toes

Oh those remote worms, my toes. I
have never included them in *me*.
Yes, I have touched them sometimes, to
improve health of *me* — to powder
them and manicure their grotesqueries;
but I have never seriously included
them in *me*. I must! because it
is apparent, they are attached. I
find, late enough, it is better
to regard them as my family than
my sons and daughters who run away and,
if angers rise, slander. (That is another
part, tongue, not nearly as trustworthy
      as toes). They are my soldiers:
can deliver a rough kick, or
messages, without protest. Tip-a-toe, I
remember now, too, they are my secret
agents, spies who aid and abet my
eyes. Never, in future, shall I neglect their
drill — such a redoubtable squad. Each
morning I shall have them bow and rise to
me, and spread like the sun's rays.
      I believe that I should
think about them in preference to the
members of my family. With toes, I
may tip-toe out into a new
      world of realisation.

# The Fourth Vowel

One letter only, only
one letter describes Earth, its
adulation — O
                    and no
letter adds knowledge, however
it may be involved. Always a
world of surprises devolves about
O.
        Difficult to keep it out.
Always that intrusive O
on our tongues.

        I would learn a language
without O, if I could. Straighten
its perimeter, as does Oriental
script. Goodness! even in the
description of my desire, I must
include O.

        O in the Occident, O in the
Orient . . . O World! were you a
flat space still, without that
heretic, Columbus, to roll you up.

        Living on you would have
been more exciting. Imagine
the dread of flight over the
edge of the world.
                    O wonderment!

# Answers

carefully telling me the answer . . .
as though it mattered, when answers
come after, are hindsight, which
don't matter except to an
inebriate TV audience, or
to schoolteachers.

                    To claim that
I could have avoided my condition
had I known that bottles which are
green contain poison! I am
colour-blind. You will have to
stage other answers — a whole shelf
of them — and I may be interested
if you do.

                    As for convictions that
follow: again — a retinue, hangers-on,
fag-ends to reason.

                    Tell me a
new story beginning . . . I am all
ears for the happening event, have
been trying to trap one
                    all my life.

# 'Do You Plan a Poem?'

'Do You Plan a Poem?'
he asked me '. . . plan a poem?'

Dial a prayer? Walk upstairs
when the parson says! How,
when these many voices tell
me: write this word, stage this
phrase? No. Too late for
planning.
         Lives cycle, all,
around emotions. Don't
believe the planner: man who's
never touched the wind ahead
and known the crashing gates it
springs and doors it slams, and
walls it builds and breaches;
or the vacuum when it has
blown itself out in the damaging
storm — come the calm.

Such affront! when I don't know or
ask the will that guides my pen;
knowing not a line ahead,
except a poem — what it's said
so far — how far?

Shall the inspiration cease? Shall
the peace of mind return? Shall
I hate the days I'll wait until
I'm willed again to write?
Keep it short? Cut the poem?

I don't know and fear always
an ending when there's ink
enough, but fingers of a
planner, only, for the poem.

# Professional Poets

I don't know about them, having
written (*my way*) over a half century of
ink; and that's a mileage I
wouldn't care to untravel.
                              If
the gentlemen (but, then, they could scarcely
remain so, and still act as professionals)
appear, unfortunately my poems (paid
for only at a pittance towards the begrudged
expenses of an amateur) won't fund me
to go to see the magisterially great
. . . certificated, associated.
                              See
I haven't the vocabulary. They'd
tutor me, if I were younger and
showed promise; but, being
aged, I can't have talents which would
promise. Youth holds that monopoly.

Hoi, there. Hoi! I saw a professional's
had atop the tallest building on a
campus. If I were a robin, I'd
fly and moult a feather in it;
no pigeons' crap left, like that, here,
I am excreting in my amateurish
wobble of a strut, seeking comparisons.

Are you an amateur and dare write a
poem? Hide it, hide it! here comes
that most knowledgeable professional poet.

# On Writing Elegies

How convenient to find a skeleton
secure, bone-wired by fantasy,
to talk to, to clothe with your
misgivings, manipulate to ape
your faulty style. Good reason I don't
write elegies, or press, too freely,
the phantasmagoria of fame too carly
for the recently departed. It smacks of
*self* . . . self-interest to engage a caddy
encumbered with your overloaded bag.

Wind, wind aids your shots. The over-
confidence of a poor strokemaker will make
you slice; scoop and take the trophy with a
little cheating. Your caddy isn't watching.
Don't ask *me* to countersign. You've played
a game a trifle differently from
Rudyard Kipling's. You know? That man
refused a knighthood. Excellent!
He, then, reduced his handicap (to me).

A winter, after death, is my desire
to keep away the blowflies, if I fall
a little short of heaven, or the green.
At the bar, to drink to my dissuasion
to continue a bad round, to hold up
the field with elegies — post mortems
on my game.
                    Pour in your glasses all
my sorrows and laugh, laugh at a
duffer's round. It's more acceptable
in club, in company, than the new
champion's. More jokes about it.

# Balance

I don't feel secure on the cliff-walk. There
     are too many willing to agree, and,
     when we are of-one-opinion, I fear
     most for democracy. Stupid I know,
for the whole countryside of eucalypts
     and koalas will be lost otherwise.
     But whisper to Them of the concrete silos
     of flesh; they won't save their spit
     to eject from the revolving restaurant
     struggling for business, there, forty floors up.
They want to be looking out here, like me.
     Not even the Forestry officers refrain.
     Are they turned pansies? Back to the smog of the city:
     rut! grunt! buss! with no vision for me there either.

# Criminal's Child

lost in the masses of our city in
the poor opinions of
                    neighbours
    I meet a dog, barks
at me and . . .
                I fear my arrest.
But no one has ever followed me along
the street into the house of
my happiness which would defeat even
a majority of nods.
                    A child that
criminals can cherish and
be loved by, caged in
a hovel of disgust.
    I don't want you following
my thoughts, and so I have voiced
untranslatable noises to it; and
we have laughed — ha! at you. I have
taught him to spit at the wind and
dodge — yes, dodge your
                        condemnation.
    Your understanding is
all astray. Ha! there is not a
smack for him. Some day, I
expect, he will hit you hard.

# Voices

Good morning! this is the people who have died,
speaking. It isn't so bad, dead. So many
millions have tried it. You will try it, too.
We, the people, would not address you otherwise.

But in a moment, we are going to show you
a new kind of death. It is not cloud-squatting,
or the old furnace-feeding frustration.

Clean, and part of a planet, you are
going to roll amidst stars. There will be
*Time*, until we solve its conjunction with

*Space*; although we believe we're achieving
that levitation now. But you will have to
come along quickly. Good morning! this is
the people who are dead, talking. Good evening!

# The Limousine

The willows that fled past us
in our limousine are shadows
and the old bus is our hens' coop
now, blue night with pride enamels its
svelte silhouette in our backyard.

Chariots of time, old cars, sweep past
(when I believed I had to own a car, to
own you too) now dispossessed by
daybreak's poultry cackling while

I wait on two eggs for my breakfast;
going down the yard with a full
tin of scraps to find only the dupe
china egg we planted as
encouragement. Give the

old bus to them, the chooks choose
their own time for laying breakfasts out.
I'll have to park the old car now at
their convenience — as patiently
as when, lovesick, I couldn't eat.

# Bee's Sting

That was a very bad year, when
I remember the wincing visit of a
grocer — grocers visiting for orders
and thereafter payment and,
thereafter, again . . .

      but the ranunculi
were flowering almost without attention and,
pink-eyed, I realised the terror of
debt in a flowering society, where
the bees had no care, unless I foolishly
trapped one and it stung — and
when it stung, I learnt, its sting was
left in me and . . . it flew away and
died.

  I have, ever since, been considerate
of bees . . . and, our grocer was a
kind man. I didn't know why
he wasn't paid, many times; and, yet,
I ate the jam and dripping he
brought to us. Oh, I knew debt, young,
when nobody perceived it; and the
bee's sting left in me made me sorry
and soft-hearted for a loser.

      I try now
not to eat, if I owe a beggar crumbs.

# Pageantry for a
# Lost Empire
## — 1977 —

To Beatrice Davis

# Australia

Somewhat a dropped blob on a map
when considering the shape for
a continent . . . where are those brain-
like convolutions of Europe's north;
the umbilical isthmus of
the Americas; or the vast
shoulders of Asia with its
penis, India, dripping islands
into a personal ocean;
or Africa peering over
a purdah into the turquoise
eyes of a Mediterranean?

But — is this an island, or a
continent? Small enough to draft
as an island on Mercator's
Projection! Flat, raft-like, drifting
in a blue vacuum of map.

Closer — has a few features: cloud
of New Guinea (that name peeling
like old paint) heating over it.

Oh, I shudder to think I should
bring it under long scrutiny.
Its deserts may reflect, like so
many bronze mirrors wherein I'd
never see definite pictures
of myself . . .

               has been the worry of
all its inhabitants other
than its wise Aborigines
— each to sight his selfish image.

# Pageantry for a Lost Empire

Ailing spouse, brats, cows, hens, spavined
horse and cowering dog on a farm,
soil similar to a desert island's
sand, drowned in a continent's dried
sperm of space. Insular, they say
we are; but what is an island
if not a provincial jail?
Sometimes more populous than a
garret in a city — and we
share the gloom: sometimes cold rain dancing
on tin roofs to make gullies flood,
but dusty skies for months of
each year, and most seasons drought spoils . . .

a barred window opening on
the screen of an opposite brick
wall. I have never had heart to
count its bricks, though I've stared at them
and that cliché that is theirs all
day; just as unnerving as an
empty stage at midnight. Whereas
my cats are odd-looking, their eyes
are the only stars I see in
a murkiness which stares of fright. I . . .

gin for my woman! I am tired
fumbling with flies; fagged to sink in
a park's damp corner. Women will
soon forsake me. Few will sink with
me; though they were only my giggles
charmed by popping corks, and glittered
with the bubbles of champagne. Gin
for my woman now! The last

festering pit of my flagging
passion fitfully hurting . . .

bear witness to my wisdom as
an administrator. When my
country was in trouble, I was
the authority always to
apply the panacea. Who came
here first to govern? Surely
not myself . . .

I know the doctor. The doctor?
He is a friend. Is he . . . my friend?
He has predicted privately, as
befits his profession, ethics
— my demise. He guards the secret
as jealously as Cerberus . . .

soon the Rolls-Royce won't do, even
with secret guards stationed among
the crowd for my arrival at
the board-room. I must scheme for a
new one hundred million dollars
building, providing eyrie-heights
for the eagle I am; commute
in a fabled manner in a
helicopter. The business of the
corporation mustn't be hindered.
I well understand why princes
of the East once travelled on carpets
— for safe aerial conveyance . . .

my strange absence, the lull on the
stock-market may tune rumours for
another gratifying deep
recession in the economy.
I shall blow the whistle when . . .

war is not an evil when I
am in high command. I'll cut the
long hairs back, scarify the race
with death . . . my orders all from the
base camp. I'll order all to camps
of peril. No city shall be a
sanctum. Out . . . out into drill squares
all lives! Nothing private. I'll
push the spies, the provosts . . .

prayer must now follow the dead
in requiem. Balance tears, that
they don't flood and blind entirely.
Confessions . . . lists of tributes to
my little nothing I tie up
in three letters of the word, God . . .

and what of the Emperor, or
the Empress? Gold and diamonds
bustled into silk-lined crates. There
are choices — Switzerland, or the
scaffold. Peculiarly, we
secure sanctuary and a
sympathetic media . . .

and what of the Press — was the near
dissolution of an Empire there
foreshadowed? Where were the rumours?
The leaders read as somebody
desired. Opinions pressed as the
vast majority's — the people's.
Somebody even financed those
how-to-vote cards . . .

You expected from me the great
flamboyant phrases — spear-shaking
. . . at least some tub-thumping? The title

reads, 'Lost Empire!' All are pale
words now, drained of our best blood.
You would have wars, and war again?
Freight your virile young men overseas?
See! we are the old men writing
for you now. Accept our plain words.
Don't denigrate the homilies
of age. Yours the humility
as each year you age. Claims of promise
in your cries for youth echo from a past . . .

when the sun came up, they were calling for him,
Blue Collar; but he was buried under a
mountain, where a waterfall danced. His spirit was
there; but they bawled out harshly for the flesh.
They needed his shoulder to turn the wheel
to make the day profitable.
He had given weight, many times his
weight around them there on the ground
where they found his blue shirt discarded.
A woman hung it out in the sky . . .
but they called out louder, following
him; believing he would never die.
He died . . . but the blue shirt hangs there
still. It is part of a sky so many
ages have rinsed with tears. Each day
plies its worn shoulder to the wheel.

# Husband and Wife

The fool-found touch of her hand
because she smiled:
that and the irony of
tea and biscuits together . . . we!

What separates us now, but a vision
after too many séances
— the interrupting visit of outside
moonlight, a breeze of perfume and
some other's chin chucked by me.

Scheming sees a new ship launched.
I can sit in her wheel-house with a
naked toe sufficient to steer her.
For captains, new ships sail
with marital fascination . . .

but the log is a duty, becomes a
task. I query that I'll captain
another bottom of the fleet
— promote to admiral.

Sailing a solitary vessel
throughout a life has
freighted me advantages of sighting
other dream-boats, but portrays
that all bottoms buck the tides.

Never a sinecure; but this route's
voyage shrinks in leagues when
sailed so many passages.
I slip this vessel. Let the
dockmen scrape her hull.

# Last Years

So the novel years of life are
behind you! I see a spectre
in a mirror and know I greet
you with a shudder of death
in your handshake. But you are in
the skin of an ass to wait upon
Death.

Burden the breeze with a sigh,
peer out your window at mountains
of trouble? You double the skinned
ass's load as it stumbles towards
the end of the road.

Beautiful
thoughts are in the packs on its
strained back — bracelets for the
harem, silks stained by foreign skies.

I
am no prophet, but I see a
star which may develop into
your smile. Yes, the desert has the
vantage of great heights where the
heavens are like a jewel-box
at night.

If you have provender
and a sound donkey, don't fear to
travel those final leagues of age.

# Half a Loaf

My disadvantage of having
to sleep, of having to commute
to a nether world . . . isn't that
having to be content with half a
loaf? Short measure somewhere!

Spectres
have bedevilled my life. If I won't
eat contaminated bread, I
must fast alone, wasting to my
death.

Yet the miller says, flour with
no weevils is from a sterile
sack of wheat — pale, white, without
gold of sunlight.

To munch on a crust baked from that
sack is to dine on a platter
of dust — dark, darker, darkest — all
on the palate at one meal, as
fed to the still-born.

Who does not
pity them? No contrast from the womb's
conception — somewhere that breeze that
pollinated the sheath, *in absentia*.

My
disadvantage of having to sleep
is the advantage of living —
getting out of bed with my
mistress — continuing to bake a
loaf which I relish.

# Message from a Tower

I have safe news to report from
the Tower to you. If my letter
is brief, you'll know when I tell of
captures: the Tower is standing,
the dungeons are crowded, and these
are dreams I report. Could one see
a butterfly of distinction
other than moth-grey or black and
white . . . just a streak of lemon on
each wing, as if the artist could
see colour; but days ghost past, each
like a drab-winged moth.

                        The people
are chained in their old age. They live
long lives. I think some over a
century but — why do they live?
Is it to preserve an estate;
to bottle up country in vineyards,
never to have these trampled save
by elephants of neglect? And
the vineyards growing back to
a wilderness?

               We can't see the
elephants from the old Tower.
We proudly manned it years ago
in defence. Now we observe from
the Tower when we climb its stone
stairs, and stare at the countryside
where we can't see any conflict . . .

# Return to the Tower

This latest defeat when I fell
on my hands (my feet and knees at
the point of surrender) shook the whole
Tower; but there was a voice which
directed me still, to climb onto
the back of a donkey . . . and so
we made good our escape, even
though only to this lowly couch . . .

from which I could spill words, these
flooding the market place, making
dearer the cost of corn: wherefrom
I learnt that I was master of men
(with my investments here and there
in fields I had specked, like an elusive fly);

for nobody watches the fortunes
of flies, their inter-relations
— never with a fascination:
engrossed in the wicked decoy of
the lemmings, despite the exploded
theories of their suicides.

So I recline and prosper — if
called son of a maggot. Good! I
have wings that waft me to the top
of the Tower. I am back again.
What tower is so high that a
fly cannot scrape through its windows?

# In the Beleaguered City

If the diminutive is our
scale for pity, surely here my
dreams for a major structure of
delight are desolate ruins.

I was hoping to build in this
Country a massive confidence
towering through whatever clouds
gathered; but a cottage built of

uniform tiny savings here's
demolished by climate. I mush
and puddle clay when I am very
young, carry hods of the muck

for others as soon as my arms
may serve as stanchions. I must
bear up the weight of State. My fate
is indicative of the lives

of my compatriots. Never
alone in the Great Hall face to
face with a palace whore. There
are minions to drag me away,

should I aspire. Violence is
common in the Courtyard. There is
not a cobble unstained by the
blood of an insurgent. Thorough

methods of the cadre impose
penalty. If there's a little
sorrow at youth's loss, that may be
wetted with a small tear . . . to have

vapours of feeling dry this with a
quiet sigh. But a howl? That would
be mere noise of the Beleaguered
City's consummate defences.

# Tank

A reference to a tank made me
think of the old farmhouse in which
I spent adolescence.

Full of holes, but cemented to make
do, the tank wept rust yet held
the coolest, purest drink for a
hot day (if one could look away,
up-end his pannikin, remain
oblivious to tiddlers).

But . . . this armament!
reminding me
the house was burnt. New owners of
the tenure raked the ashes, rolled the
spent tank downhill to a gully
where, I dare say, the monster's
tiddlers have grown larger into
hiding snakes.

This armament rolls
round the countryside and can extend
death too, to unprotected human
flesh . . . its only purpose that I
know!

However would they name it
tank?
Not after the sacked analogy in
the gully, surely! because that
old bulk of rusting iron and
encrusting lime now harbours snakes?

Think
of the iced relief that it once
served, on summer days so mortally
hot. No other succour could relieve
the fort (and, here again, I'm not
so happy using an analogy
reminding us of wars).

# The Disarrayed

Forgetting how to observe, what
to observe, in my ageing years
. . . a rose, or a red scarf on a
young woman whom winter compels
to wear cloaking habit . . .

                         I now
recall my sisters with their dolls
and the obscenity from which
I shrank, seeing the dolls unclothed;
these looking like pullets my father
had beheaded and plucked for the
pot. Somehow the dolls always lost
their heads, or their heads seemed
        severed.

Later I thought of Gogol and
the theatre — but always this
unease in the presence of the
disarrayed.

            Imagine how I
feel now in my city's treeless
wastes strewn with the weeks' wraps
thrown down.

All such Victorian thinking!
but there is some nostalgia
for those years of my parents'
parents in the old photographs
— rich man and poor man alike in
suits, and so many rows of
women in great hats that must have

looked like gardens of flowers
to a boy climbing a tree by
the roadside, perched in a branch
above them.

Even close summer's
deep décollétes would not startle
but promise buds in spring — and who
even in those years of decorum
didn't pick bunches of rosebuds?

# Diamond

Crying for you, mother, is like
the madness of muttering in
crowds who seal the voices that the
mazed one speaks with noise and bustle,
sniggering at the tremulous
lips in passage.

                Within my heart
I heed your presence though years you
have been gone. When life has done
with me, we'll meet: together in
the purest memory Earth locks
in oceans, lands and atmospheres.
No ford of a Rubicon, no
curse of a wizard, shall press our need
to wake again with morning, to
tire in the muddled night; but each
in the impregnable diamond
shall crystallise this life, and seem
to brides and grooms the eternal
as they vow.

              Here in the vast force
of our bondage to each other,
child and mother — life and death, all
in the gem-star in long darkness
or in light of a beam's flash to
discovering eyes, be sure a diamond
rests safely within my thoughts of your
being.

        Whether that memory's mined or
I'm forgotten, the secret lies
within me — your care, your love,
your smile.

# Christmas Beetles

As I age, I have noticed a
cruelty surfacing in my once
upon a time calm nature, towards
pests. I begin to comprehend dire
excesses by dictators.

        I
have dispatched, all in one week of
early January, a whole
nation of Christmas beetles, an
Australian golden snow upon
the foliage of my garden's
eurabbie tree — the slaughter not
with the approbation of my
womenfolk who've just spent Their Year
(not without virulence either,
shown by their sex).

        Taking the place, it
seems, of some failed predator,
I've dispatched one thousand of the
insects which used to delight
me in my childhood with their all
round the room aerobatics. Gold,
indestructible when they crashed
into walls and ceilings, lending
the light their precious presence. They
were harbingers of Christmas with
its shower of gifts. I marvelled
at their manufacture from gold
and priceless jewels . . .

                              but my tall
eurabbie which they would haunt is
my pride. Their gold, a corruption
in the high palace of its branches,
is counterfeit in sunlight. They
eat into the lives of its leaves,
and I have ordered their deaths. I now
follow the laws of Nature: kill —
or have ruin my companion.

What of democracies? Half of
their populations are perforce made
dissidents, whatever faction's
in power; with no 'free' country to
which they may showily defect.

# Fallen Idol

If you were in the room, that was
where love belonged. A house was
a home then. When that presence faded
your final absence closed the doors;
the long night of my apathy
set — night beyond the reach of moons
(young breasts) where I would rest a hand
on yours . . . after, a prisoner's life
in stone.

       Time picked me up and skittered
my fragments on sleep's mirrored waters
— each fracture of that statue which
I posed. Before, there was such magnitude
the room seemed light and expansive. You
and I could triumph across, as
though this were the world's map.

                     After
my witless plea at our parting.
I'd fared better sinking to the bed
of a lake (being that my skip from
love and life). Though such fiction may
amuse some Power, such losses
I have suffered to forsake a
room lie moodless as a stone
at the bottom of grief's dark sea.

# Deities

I could conceive of a God who
loved perfection; but never of a
monster-warrior in the skies
warring upon mortal mores,
to bend to this will or to that.

A God I'd talk with would live on the
Earth, as I ever amazed at
beauties of far constellations,
their likenesses in the countless suns
that breach upon a wave inshore.

I'd differ from him, when I chose
a colour and, through diffusion, we
would paint again the perfect smile.
The wonder, never mine alone,
this God would be the artist, not

the cancerous scientist who
tugs the Universe apart. No
need for deeper scrutiny than
a child's! That would be his first and
last love of creation: to

touch, to smell, to taste, to hear and
see; quite undisturbed by nightmare,
living in the day, loving each
tumbling second beautiful in
the waterfall — last, to look up
to see the stream was Life.

# The Dream

Here is the dream that filled no time
but a wink of sleep and then woke
me with a yelp of fear: that I
should die . . . others were immortals.
Yes! I had blundered into the
company of devils and of
angels. They'd burrowed or breezed
even to this Australia.

Some emerged through the charred bark
of trees, the gargoyle rocks of
the hills. The angels flew as
such a profusion of birds, I knew
they'd brought God's memories here.
Still some were petrified in stone
masonry, permanently perched
on St Carmel's Convent which
I passed along my track to school . . .

The convent children grimacing
at me, because I wasn't of
the Faith . . . their parents, too, held mine
in ostracism for the 'flaw', I
noticed. Latterly, in age, no
ease, compunction in us as grown
men and women. Let's face up! we
still throw stones over a convent
wall; and these are bits and pieces
of the devils of my dreams. Sometimes
a nun steps out, crying: 'Children!
Children! will One die and not all?'

# Old Jack/Young Jack

Old Jack/Young Jack: they're back home
together again. Sometimes one sees in the
old man's eye the devil-may-care
whence young men die. Sometimes men see
in his smile old transmutations of
silver to gold which Jack needs spend
to the end of his days in praise of
the World that spins him round to
Young Jack from Old Jack — Yes, back
again to Young Jack! It seems now,
as here he squats most of his days
in a cane chair, one friend alone is
visiting him — Young Jack to Old
Jack . . . here with his smile visiting him.

## The Muscovy Duck

The white duck came to us, flying,
we deduced, into our garden
at night, or when our attentions
were diverted: which must seem much
of time to our garden — or does
our absence mean nothing there?
No message, note of ownership
under the duck's white wings. So we
became friends, offering it plates
of mash; and, with the far-seeing
eyes of a duck, it possessed us.

How do you put off a friend out
of nowhere? We couldn't describe
this as a lost bird. Have there
ever been such fallen avian
souls, other than fledglings found sprawled
from unguarded nests in the caves?

To name it was our necessity;
but that name flew away with it
after months of companionable
acquaintance: at which point of our
friendship we felt let down by
the sky which returned our gaze of
loss and self-questioning with a
blasé blue stare of nothing more
to say about departures, but
some deference to a duck's-death;
for it may have glimpsed that end in
our eyes beyond the proffered plates
of bran.

What did we eat? Duck? We
had no such ideas on this
tourist; but all ducks look beyond
ideas. Try to stalk ducks on
a wide waste of water! They are
more cautious than seagulls with the
gulls' boundaries set at a half
beach's latitude of escape.

                              Just
as we've proved unsafe friends (for
we are raconteurs) maybe
the duck was wise to take flight from
people who spoke in one's absence.

# Stroll Down a 'Closed' Jetty

I walked the jetty back, following
a past; watched with suspicion for
my trespass on the staggered deck
beyond an ominous red sign . . .
'WARNING' . . . a seal upon neglect.

Progress doesn't march my jetty,
left for the sea's removal by
occasional busy-bees of
tempests.

What a jeweller's shop
seen through windows of missing
planking! Those frames showed me gems
I could possess, but at the price of
life and this was just as valued
now as in my youth — more so, as
I had less to squander of the
substance. I saw the clarity
and all the colour that is life's.

An ad. for this — the sea had strung
a necklace of pearl-winged seagulls
round a sandy cay. That string was
safe offshore away from land and
all disturbances of traffic:
shelved and more noticeable than
upon a neck of land
however slender.

# Flight of the Waterfowl

. . . and the thin reeds swayed like
tired worms yawning, and the Earth's
vocal poets spoke in vain. Was this their
song: freedom of a breeze across a marsh
. . . good fortune? . . . final tragedy of an
abandonment to swans and geese
without the record of a word?

I think the Word was Silence here
to all the tongues of all the nations of
the Earth, had taken refuge here
and here was its seclusion from
a sense of weariness that left
the armies bogged in bitter contest
along the margins of the skies'
expanse — horizons out of sight of
'Peace'.

         Whoever sought it? Who
of all the human tripe, apart from
those lonely individuals
who came here to die, to sink in
sad admission of the human bog . . .
while swans and geese flew overhead
using the kindest movement of
the heavens (for such use, angels
blessed their winged souls, saw time was
better left with age to marry
the absent and the present in one
pact of being).

So in the swamp
if one had built a lowly cot
of reeds, he too might tour the
heavens with the leader of
the swans and soar without a
moment's consternation to his star.

# Ghosts

*for my granddaughter, Lindy Melly, Vancouver, B.C.*

Ghosts: blanched memories seen
eerily through a lack of flesh, with
rag their only substance pegged on
height. Yes, ghosts are very tall and
pegged up. So few of their audiences
picture a tiny ghost. Such would seem a
rag doll of infancy. No . . . they're tall
towering over us; their size
casting their jellied spells from a shambles
of features which are vaguely memorised as
the embroidered holes in valances where
moths have munched . . .

                       and theirs is a semblance
of the draped shapes of moths with their red
eyes; and moths are, perhaps, the missing
diminutives of small ghosts. With
a dash of colour in their capes
and day's largesse, they could flit
by as butterflies do in sunshine and
be loved by all — and whoever is
terrified of a colourful butterfly?

# A Ball Game

Only last season there was a
screen of forest where the hill is
bald; which means I see the sun rise,
the sun set, seconds earlier
or later, according to which fall
of the hill I camp on. I don't
bother to make an issue of
this, as a conservationist
with clangour of protest. I
accept the changing face of life;
realise life passes away
not only for eucalypts on
a ridge, but for all life on the
Earth's verge. What else is the surface
of a sphere?

             Hang on with your feet!
Were you an insect you might find
that to station yourself on a
leaf — eight legs, antennae pointing
to stars — easier, comfortable.

I feel this my hardest task: to
stand up, point two legs downwards and
reach up for stars. Some defect as
the dinosaurs experienced
— my sort of life cannot be of
an order that will be accepted
on Earth for ever. I am
failed, like the dinosaurs. Life for
me is terminal (brilliantly
adapted word of the day).

My child's
children I forsake to live with
auguries. When the hills' soil slides
away, youth must climb precipices
of rock revealed. Only the stars
will hang through the years overhead;
and eyes may not see them for
the smoke of tree-stumps burn out
and the dust from a slide of soil.

Such evolutions will affect this
planet until it hangs quiet
in the heavens as a puzzling
silent moon. There will be some act for
Earth to play mysteriously
in the chaos I can perceive.
Just stamping me out won't cancel
Earth and the skies.

If it's replays
I'm waiting for, these were destroyed.
A ball game will continue in
the heavens without Earth's viewers.

# Turned Out

Have I raced this far, at last to
be turned out in vast paddocks
of prose: the thoroughbred poet
nibbling at stubble, out of his
box of verse? To what point I sped
round the circuits carrying boys
and weights to the disapproval
of . . . well, mothers and children starved
as I sprinted and stopped in the
straight. There were boos for me too when,
seldom, I did get up, only
because of the dead 'uns I passed.
Editors, sports editors, smell
'cold decks'; but they write no abuse.
They flee to the whisky bar, pat
the trainer's back and say, 'Good colt
that'; overlooking that I've been gelded
and it's my last run.

                    Into
the paddocks of drought and despair:
my bones to whiten like scraps of
paper which I've ruined with verse.

# Anthology

Each poet playful with a train
of thoughts running along the
spiked track, bypassing at a loop,
where loop of metaphor or
simile makes one line or the
other interchangeable
directions . . .

               analects to
extend a train's length. How many
can the poem pull through Bulli
Pass, or sneak into a tunnel
of smoky obscurity?

                 Best
wait on the platform with all the
scholars. There is a timetable
to which each train is scheduled for
a workaday appearance . . .

                         of
a crush of tame poetasters.

# Burnt Poems

They said, the Japanese burnt poems.
Insuperable the loss. How much
ash is burnt poems? Whole cities
burn. Are there no poems in them?
I've burnt so many volumes: some
written, unwritten — these latter
crammed with the invaluable works.

All prices are inflationary
if you pay them. They're down at mouth,
and drop if you pass by.

                    Let's do
just that to panegyrics from
the critics, unless they've true gold
offering, on display — at least
an ingot for bare eyes to sight,
assay.

        We may get taken in
by highly polished brass. At least
we've felt a weight of metal.
We know values,
drop dross back to grass.

# New Ground

If you don't make a noise and then
suddenly you speak, even your
friends take fright; may pay you back with
sentence, reserved by courts for sneak-
thieves. Is that my thunder upsets
you too? An old Chinese clangour
to frighten the spirits that run
before one, or honking geese, are
better welcomed. Night can defer
dark station to the dawn; but a
mind that's unaware is afraid
of new knowledge unless the mind
be that of an explorer.

                    Now,
take stock of your courage, your bragged
avant-garde position. The dogs
bark with such trepidation at
the unknown suddenly in their
scent. They have noses for the strange
and bark their warning. Are you by
your reaction registering
fear of my intrusion, too?

No doubt! although
I'm here, friend, for
identification of my
person. I spoke too suddenly?
Don't discuss my entrance for, I
believe, I found you sleeping fast.

# Story of an Uncle

He sat never without a hat
at table, an old Irishman
of temper, a determined Jew of
custom; and, whoever blew in,
'Sit down,' he said. He always sat;
and how objects came to him at
table was explained by the small
dimensions of his one room shack.

Sit down! You did — on his doorstep
and at your feet the tread of the
beach and a wide blue carpet of
sea (cleaner for you to visit
on fine days) were the stairway and
grand hall of his domicile . . . as
well, that room under his hat where
he stored old masters. I never

forget one lurid Turner, one
morning after a night of rum
and whatever debauch he could squeeze
into his shack. 'Come back, Jack,' he'd
apportioned the morrow . . . a fat
harlot giggling inside and I,
a young fellow, wouldn't wait to hear
the cats yowling in the coal black
density of night. (He was the
miner . . . the canary was in
his pit, I too young to descend
shafts. The pitheads looked stark enough.)

I would return when he emerged to
the light of day. He was never
ashamed, but cautionary to
me; and silently I thanked him
without words where he meant these words:
'Never go down the mine, nephew!'

# Photographs

I have given up taking photos. They,
most, group me with old-timers. Grey
scripts, old ghosts act out. Even the
newer coloured prints, heavenly
though the backgrounds, show me up as a
monster emerging from a miasma
of verdure — I invariably choose the
backgrounds of hedges or a low tree,
squat, unpruned, as I look ill-groomed.
Even in those photos where flowers bloomed
I have not disguised my ashen face
except in one likeness which I hide, posing
in an archway of some dingy place,
as a clown with cherry nose, crossed dozing
eyes, and a white powdered complexion;
there, in character, framed to perfection.

# The New City Poems
## — 1980 —

To Patrick White

# On a Breath

Myself! he laughs. He's living just
back of my nose, thin walls between
him and my ears and an easy
view from my eyes.

Pops in and out
on each breath and can stay away . . .
could stay away!

Too temporal for the rent he pays my
carcass; but he's a tenant I like
so let live on.

I'll eject him when he gets too
late coming home some night — if the
local corpus doesn't rule him
out bodily with force before the
expiry of his lease. That
concerns me more than him!

I can
imagine him going out on
a breath.
Which wind he'd take to the sea or
which to the mountains, would have me
mystified.

I could look only up at the
sky, transfixed on my skeleton.
The corpus would rule, 'Make no more
bones about it', and smother me
in my grave.

# The Picture at Graham's Place

What a party we had for Sheila . . . in
that round-about jolly picture where
nobody asked which way but went along
and met a face, or a figure, or
came to a building of a soft and
unpretentious style which held our
laughter without a cackle and
none of the lies of echoes.

Joy meant there, as in the outdoors,
where eyes met without demur in
naked colours.

    Imagining back
I can't remember a shadow
or one sun lording the skies with
a penchant to rule direction.
We went along. The world was a
smile, as I dreamt.

We sat around and, when we looked
into the picture without hard rules
of composition, we sensed there . . .
laughter, laughter!

    We saw there
Sheila's charm.

# The Poet's Page

I told them about the loneliness of
the page the blank white page; how nobody
had smudged the smooth paper, or dog-eared the
sheet . . . and I faced into a snowstorm that
misted out of the blanched forests and spread
its dazzle of white to obscure vision.

There were young faces in the silent
audience and I could not see one, yet
I spoke to all about the fear of the
white page — the blizzard to brave through travail.

I lurched towards them till within ear-shot
of my name, so that they might bury me with
knowledge that I had been human, snow-shoeing
far till they discovered I'd been printing a
trail . . .

            perhaps one of the faces had discerned
that the cold page was being traversed by
me — I had written this strange poem to
them . . .

            perhaps they had faced the blizzard — woman
or man. Either would have been alone, but
approaching me . . . approaching me . . . Yes! We
would have stared singly, then together
at loneliness of the white page for the
poet — some sort of triumph in our eyes;
a gleam that remained, light-frozen, snow-blind.

# Houses and Homes

Houses and homes were important in my
youth. Now I am at home in the wilderness —
by which I mean, not the bush or the city,
but among the bewildered.

                           Homes are where
my mother resided. The houses — later
domicile? She lives in my memory
and I am at home. The big houses — the
big homes? My father liked rooms about him.

My mother was a cottager at heart . . .
and I? I have lived in the heart and found
that place warm and cold by degrees as graded
as the front and back stairs. Most of our
residences were of timber, on stumps; but
that last big house had to be brick, I
believe, because brick smothers sounds and
parents can argue beyond the family's hearing.

Not understanding a heart's breakages
(my own, intact, beat off the clutch of death)
I learnt that hearts break up in marriages;
though my two parents were never divorced.

Both held their pride of which I was not proud,
but am glad to remember now. There were
no losers, no brutalities — but words . . . and
how separate are their meanings!

                           I play
with words here, again to remind you, there is
distinction between a house and a home.

# The Leopard-ash Tree
*for Judith Wright*

This year became widowed of the
leaf of the leopard-ash tree. In
the fall, our autumn too sees the
shedding of leaves. The leopard-ash
bares wire-like twigs, enticements for
the lightning of spring; and when that
season breaks, the new-born leaves are
red as hour-old babies. They still
huddle, their hands screwed tight as
leaves can curl.

        My obligation is
to observe and not chop out what
may have seemed a dead tree, dead to
all futures.

        Life has left all memory in
the sap and when the blood moves up
in the summer florid faces
will cool their brows under a new
green foliage.

        There will be
golden flowers again as the
light-green leaves take hold of
the sun and capture warmth in a
velvet sheen, deepening towards
summer evenings' shades, clothing
the mature tree.

# As a Dead Bird

I own books like it, which I've shelved.
I wonder whether the grey lice
will devour their pages and they'll
strew embarrassment when they
are plucked from my bookshelves — like
a dead bird's feathers . . .

                              and there will
be no contents that I remember.

Title . . . name? Yes, I recognise
the species, its particular
loping flight — too laborious
to follow.
              Cat and roach may prey
on it (my all-seeing cat
that seems to see through the leaves
of a forest to spot a bird;
kills it, not for the flavour).

                              I
had such habits of reading, once;
and those books not lent for ever
remain like dead birds.

                         I would
not disturb them with finger
or toe. Let them rest, or fear their
untidy disintegration.
As dead birds, they'll spirit
away in time far out of mind.

# Once I Wrote a Book

The book contained the secrets of
my hopes abducted, imprisoned, scorned
in unmannerly fashion by
the uninterested. It was
full of geese in flight, swans on the
waters and some pelicans for
funny men. Yes! its subjects
migrant as waterfowl. Perhaps
some saw a tide's bookmark at low ebb
leaving the pages soggy, yellowed
and rimpled.

But he who reads may see here imprints
as on a seabed when the tide rolls
out . . . perhaps as child or poet
sees the waves in minuscule
on the sands and bothers to pause
admiring the pattern . . .

                                    did God here
fingerprint the escaping tide . . .
toe-prints of the Deity's Son
who had walked on the waters?

Pages full of such lore. If my
book lies stolen, unread on a
thief's desk, I pledge to him more than
this quill of the contents; because
a book is a fond memory . . .
a bank of memories. Dunes of them
shored up against the inrush
of tides of the forgotten.

# Autobiography of an Antithesis

*If he has one figure behind him (and I do not suggest any
influence) it would be Thomas Hardy.*

— Review

I am happy to say that I haven't
read his poems. I would fear to be
discovered reading them in the shade of
his Greenwood Tree; to learn that I was
as ingenuous as he. Yet I have
bought a volume of these words. I fear
to read them, to find that they may be more
than words — strike from the page at me, stab
my flesh with their meanings, leave me
wounded from the loss of thoughts I could
not then retrieve from prized origins
which I'd conceived were mine.

               Such vessels
as my veins, I fear, would be sapped;
as words, eavesdropped in this review, bled
from my heart indulgences I could not stem.

His volume is close on my shelves and
remains closed. Out of opinion
I conclude this judgment final
as sentence that, should I read his lines,
I shall not write again. My thin voice will
be his. Mine will be words alone, without
a purpose for using words at all.

# Hang-gliding

No man can experience that
sheer delight, unless he has stepped
off a precipice and is a
capable hang-glider; and then
he mustn't wonder whether he
looks impressive to anybody
above or below, or looks like
an over-size fruit-bat in splints,
a big eagle hanging around
in pyjamas in daytime, or
just some kid's blue plastic kite caught
in high tension wires . . . for viewpoints?

Vantage points! Manna for which
tourists pay up, detouring to find
a leaving of existence
other than
always . . .

            just a step off into
the much-photographed, but
must-be-experienced view of
a place where heat and flies are not
on postcards.

Who are the weaklings who fear to be
such sightseers? A dull genus, beings?

Come away with us for views. See
the hang-glider. Who sees the views
better than the hang-glider boy?
Soon, very soon, a whole season
of hang-gliders . . .

            Open to guns?

# Placenames

On a bike, I once explored the
wonderful; riding the country
roads, perched on two O's. Those days of
dirt tracks under eucalypts
are now struggles to remember
because, then, I had nothing to
forget; but lived the whole journey
through clear daylight without a
sluggish sleep to sop in Lethe's
flow. The names of little towns which I
passed through I can't remember now.
There were too many English names,
Scottish, Welsh and Irish; though the
country was Australia's. (There
rings an alias in that name, too?)
Sometimes Aboriginal names
were music to me; but after my
ears' shock at hearing lyrical
Jenolan derived from J.E.
NOLAN, I never noted names
of places, but travelled while I
was still entranced enough by all I
saw, with aid of the two O's
transporting me. I sold my bike
to a man named J.E. NOLAN.

# Empire
*for Patrick*

Where we ran without shoes and the
weeds stung like winter, we didn't
mind the pain; we were young and
though school was on our way there was
the rest of day stacked high with the
golden hours of games we pilfered
from the planes of poverty. From
meals of bread and jam we succoured
energies of sweetness enough
to give us speed to run from home.

There were truants plentiful and
wild among us who ran away to
toil, and grew old as men within
our teens; for work was everywhere:
along the roads to build, and scrubs
to fell. They savaged us, sweated
us to build an Empire and why
we did we never asked, but died:
some in the mines, some clerks in
narrow offices. Always for little
profit and an Empire's gain.

Those of the lucky few who
escaped to sea as sailors we
never met again; imagined
them as rulers of the waves — fed
back such rumours. Over all, the
Crown behind the glass of distance,
safe as a cottage pie which we
never tasted, never could consume;
our diet brackish with our sweat,
our blood the wine of profiteers.

# Reflections on an Accident

While they won't run with me now, I
find those willing bearers, my
legs, glad to carry me down a
quiet street, avoiding the fast
traffic of swollen freeways. Where
they leisurely stroll me, a few
eucalypts come back in focus
standing among houses. I'd
thought all forests were down; but while
some trees stand in leaf I can see
structures that support more than smoke
in the skies; blossoming a host
of May Gibbs Bib and Bubs with noise
of nursing bees mothering the
long-eyelash babies among the
star-thronged branches — tumbling, never
falling hurtfully upon the
earth beneath spread with its lace of
sunlight and shadow.

                    I'd thought their
avian orchestras had long
ago disbanded, but they are there:
an insect hum to accompany
solo, duet, of songbirds . . . a
robin, or a bush canary
attacking the high notes; friar-birds
miming traffic's cacophony.

Whether my temporary
deprival of a car is a
good accident with no injury
except to the ego of metal
and paint, I am sure I won't spill
glass tears in the quiet street, as
my car wept its at the scene
of the accident on an over-
thronged highway. My legs bear witness
to a new mobility, disprove
the fallacy of a shrinking
planet, Earth. Car-less, I find I'm
careful and not careless of the
values of a vicinity
and, suddenly, turn naturalist.

# Fossil Man

The tired nerves of my brain tangle,
touch and fuse into lethargy;
my body aches under the weight
of a calcified cranium.

Relief to ease me into sleep,
to dream my sleep will trade with death
the petrified mind.

                Centuries
may be days until the team of
archaeologists lets me see
light again, digs me out (my thoughts
inviolate, my theories not
disproved).

             There is a set firmness
about my closed jaws goes with the
face. All is conjecture as to my
praise or ridicule of these men:
they'll too wish peace of burial.
Who will seek their bones?

                  Their
radium-singed remains may in
an equal period of death
upset the carbon clock in its
determination of their ever
having existed.

            Their atoms,
being too active, many disperse in
sleep. Death may never be a
solid state again.

# Murray River Cod

The paddle steamer plies the course many hundred voyages, but I have been able after each passage to sit upon the riverbank, on a red-gum log and look at the image of my face over the reeds, coolly, calmly. The image isn't me, but a likeness which embodies all the lassitude I feel on a hot day under the trees' shade by the river. Narcissus haunts me. I have been audience for many years to my own image and see no change except more ripples on my visage after each transient vision of the river-boat. I return to calm, my face the mirror of my soul. My ethos shines. Boats are few between my visits to the river that mirrors me as steadfast native company. Narcissus haunts the river. I fish there more patiently than the kingfisher, or the egret, each of whom I see recognise the spirit of the stream drawn out as a tiny silver sliver from the water — a likeness to a piece of broken mirror. My fish, for which I may wait days or weeks, will bear a different likeness . . . a whirlpool of a fish that swirls and weaves towards the reeds. I must not let him escape the terror of the sun's face high above him, to tangle in a beard of reedy anonymity, hence be forgotten. I must become active as the suns dancing on the steamer's wake, to steer him from the reeds and lay the gasping image of all flesh upon the riverbank.

# A Foggy Morning

The morning's fogged heavily. The only colour, apart from the depthless silver, on which my eyes open is the pink of the oleanders that rise outside my window, instead of the sun. Should the sun never rise, I have no care. Let the pinkness be substitute for sunlight. Outside, is the silver foliage of my spinning-gum, a tree that fills one half of my casement window with leaf that's independent of gross wooden limbs, but follows where leaves blow upon a wind, suspended in silver filigree. Is this the morning because my conscious state returns? True I have heard the exploring tenor of the silver-eyes, knowing these tiny birds can sense this is the hour when suns should rise. They wake to song without the beckon of the sun. Here is a time when they and I appear in refuge from day's common stare. All is so still and the silver-eyes are singing of our anonymity. They are not querulous of clocks. For me — a key to silence, their pitch of song. If other lives can't wake today, I shall enjoy my preference of silver. Always I've treasured silver more than gold, not bargaining about the market's values. The fog makes slugs of people who sleep on. I am the solitary bidder for a silver day hammered with tiny notes into this silver-plate by the silver-eyes' singing in the oleanders' wake of pink.

# Afternoon and Evening — Gataker's Bay

I watch the water. Idly I sit under the pandanus palm seeking shade until the shoreline's traverse widens beyond the beach and blends with the solidity of night. How venture on this stage — to find the dancers absent? The ballet of the waves has vanished. In the black east a hushed noise of assembly only (departing Dogberries). Not even a garment of light forward of the proscenium of nightfall. I've stayed too long, alone and late; and no moon is billed to appear. The shoreline links a tideless scallop of bays as I stroll up the headland . . . all seats are thrown back, the flat floor of each bay's theatre is vacated by the shining audiences of planets, stars, meteors, which I have known reflecting in a customary evening's enchantment. Clouds pall across the sky. Water will soon become a personal sweat of reckoning on my bare head, soaking me through. I have noticed at low tide: rain . . . often rain at the ebb of light . . . and in what company? All whom I may meet: a few cowled priest-like fishermen choosing the gloom for their avowed purpose as I seek refuge.

# The Medusa

I'd like to hide, but cannot hide my vision of the bay's incoming evening tide behind a stiff nor'easter; standing at the head of English echo-named Sandgate's storm-racked pier, upon a fo'c'sle which, like a ship's, savours the gale. Looking down aghast, in wonder at the changing scene . . . lost memories of youth. Flood of a biscuit-coloured sea, brick-coloured combers purling with a scum of yellow soup atop and, in the tide, appearing as the hooded ghosts of ocean, the only blue reminders of an oncoming sea, the 'blubbers' (how here preserved so blue?). Jellyfish a foot across the dome . . . equivalents of human heads with, under each, a mouth grotesquely stuffed with, what appear to me, blue thick fingers of incumbent idiocy. Here is a scene, I won't go away and forget . . . those blue shapes! Here is the sea baiting me with infelicities of colours. Shall eyes turn purist and give praise to 'blubbers' — the sea a mockery of colour for which the sea was ever praised? I've never welcomed sight of 'blubber' on the tide before this humid summer evening's grey defeat of a blue sky, smothering with off-shore smog (not spume) the sun's last function of the day . . . the Medusa welcomed here as sea's last mockery of the legendary Gorgons. What mermaids! Don't blind yourself to change to these unnatural colours, but gaze awhile with me and let your mind be numbed . . . let the Medusa brush against your brain.

# Close-ups

I take the view from Mount Parnassus and
see what I expected . . . always from mountains
viewing the expected: small towns, silver
threads of streams, the diminutive buildings, the
figurines of a remote existence . . .

Squashed in a room with you, I touch, I scent,
I clasp and stare at parts of you; so close
I can't see more than your breasts sometimes
perhaps your eyes — the personal parts of
life that make me roll over on tourist
brochures on my bed and crush Switzerland.
Weren't the Alps formed by some such thoughtlessness?
I climb more than Mont Blanc at a leap. I
don't go to Switzerland, but marry you.

# So Like My Young Mother

October, the weeks of Libra, in this
year '78 (born 1913) still
with hooks to my eyes, philandering
in a beach-front motel, charged an outrageous
tariff at Mermaid Beach . . . hearing fat mermaids,
size of big waves, flop over all day, all
night; next a neighbour so like my young mother:
strangely met in old age . . . and I look at her
with her several kids already; and
she smiles her young mother's smile at me, so I
turn to her as 'poor little boy' once more and
the hooks drop from my eyes. My smile for her must
beam nearly a simper of recognition
of ageless, unrehearsed filial devotion.

# If You Seek Poetry, Avoid

the Poets. Search for the quiet
peace that waits under a stone: a
fern's or a lichen's, that will sleep
through fall in the spore, until . . . If
you are a poet, wait until
you are asked to read your poem
(perhaps when you are deceased, or
have desisted from writing all
poems). Travellers report that the
desert's a place of poetry . . .
because there is no alternative.
Death may be its state poets seek.
After they disappear, hollow
bleached skulls may recite their poems.

# The Actor

I hadn't expected to be
cast in the role of an old
man walking city streets so soon.

Look at all the young ladies!
Or are they actresses who
play parts of anonymity?

I'd like to cast them, lovers, each
with a bouquet I presented
every hour of my life;

billing each and every one
a star . . . each bouquet a hair of
my old grey locks refreshed by the

dews of love — I, a young man
again . . . but no. I have played the
part of lover as have other

men. These are their daughters upon
whose beauty my eyes trespass. I
must hobble on, hand on heart, in

search of a park bench whereon
I may resume my act of age,
play out my role of old man.

# To Roland Robinson

Roland, having never met before, you
were a new book to me. Yes . . . I
had read your poetry; but
a person should always be less
than his poems, as any man at
a point in time is the fraction
of his being.

        He knows time's
triumphs and betrayals compute
He has a credit or loss to
show balance of mind.
               I've thought
the betrayals sub-total into
us. The columns of triumphs are riches
so temporarily possessed.

I had no idea of your accounting
until we met in Adelaide in
early March.

        March — what connotations!
That month pings arrows from the taut
bowstrings of the centuries.

            Even so,
we met in corps, naked in character
to each other's eyes; and I sensed
immediately that we stood foot
to foot in the same phalanx with
the ceaseless enemy arrayed
against us.

That was a strange sense
to bring to mind in twentieth
century Australia; but,
having met, I believe that time and
place were peradventure: we
scanned the trivia which our laurelled
imperator expected of us.

# In the Garden

Thinking too harshly of the late
years is a young man's folly: his
vanity handed mirror and
brush. Whereas I realise such
kind days I haven't known before
when I could watch the wood-doves
and the pied shrieks shuffle around
a dribbling garden hose.

                         Doves in
quiet patience, alerted by
each moving shadow; the shrikes that
we call butcherbirds (accepting
their plain truce for the present) are
thirsting, not for blood, but water
on this occasion. Prey and
predator compund where thirst rules, so
I see.

         My thirst for life is still
a young man's though now I drink with
doves, forgetting obligations
to quaff that stronger brew among
the shrikes that visit flesh-pots,
like great bullies in their idle hours.

Yes, I liken young men to the
shrikes whom I see butchering the
frightened grey-winged hours of peace.

# Winning Post

At the finish there was a post
stolid and wooden and standing
alone with the winner who had
left his friends for company of
a post.

      Strung out behind him,
the retinue developing
sympathy, forming company,
they began unwinding, laughing
at their failures, ignoring
the finish once the race was run.

The post held no significance
more than a timber obstruction
to be drawn from the earth, dragged
away as lumber.

           The winner
tried to merge back with people,
but had to part company
first with the post whom he had thought
an important companion where
he might lift a leg any time.

# Pottsville

We could have peopled Pottsville, watched
the birds there stand on stilts built like
the houses of the beautiful-limbed
negresses whose
                        heads carried the
weight of matter of life and whose
black backs were straightened by balance
through long carriage of many dark
centuries of African solace.

Pottsville! Where, as a tourist, I
saw genuine smiles like peeled bunch-
ripened bananas, and devoured
a tongue swollen for love . . .

                                Love
simple for those people devoid
of obsequious delays. Brats laughed
with bride and bridegroom . . .

                        My forebears
grumbled once, 'The Civil Service
cannot hold us here. Bah! Africa!'

Australia, their different dish; where
lash of whip wouldn't provoke
a spear in the back through felt-hot
walls of cane. No! If not English
stone, they'd have felon flesh to hew
rock walls to grey conformity.

As the past's tourist, were I my
father's father, there'd been little
heed to gape at race and colour.

I'd have been dropped between two tall
shapely legs, flies unseen on a
dark countenance; have watched all
day the tall stately birds
stalking locusts . . . gathering from
infancy life's fascination.

# The Gate-keeper

## I

I was standing at the gate. I am still
standing there, as time remembers, though
action has transpired. I am waiting for an
arrival, or departure: some more detailed
tedious information of motion.

I prefer the still, graphic picture of
my standing at the gate.
                              Seconds ago
that was the station of my memory
and that pose, all I saw, remains somewhere in
mind.

        Yes! there were comings and goings of
importance to some people, but I stood
there and must stand there for old people
who keep servants.

                        While they live,
shadows stage — motionless of lip and eye.

The scene needs no repair, no thought for
after-life. I was, I am standing at the gate:
a memory of position I can't shift for them —
tiresome though my stance may seem.

# II

A goat is tethered near and pokes his head
between rail and crossmember, to nibble my
white pocket-handkerchief which flaps beside
his tuft of beard.

                  I think this makes the goat seen
as some ancient mandarin. I am in
élite and timeless company —
the mindless posted guard for a fragile
mandarin midst all his silks and porcelain;
drilled not to move, not open — shut the gate
lest time shake down the shelves of china
and let the palace sway towards an open space,
with dark winds blowing towards nowhere known.

# A New Day's Sun

One of those breeds of fowls that clutch
onto, hatch out, a nest of eggs — leaving
finally one embryo swarming with
ants — to strut off with the brood of a
dozen chickens all destined for
the pot . . .

              but (who knows) may be the
champion hen's or cockerel's coop
as the royal exhibition for one
with a purple card and a gold
tasselled ribbon draped over the wire.

Not for me! Do I exist only for the
family lineage? Do I live at all
outside the likenesses of photographs
of too many generations?

                  'Isn't
he like . . .'

I shall cut off an ear,
like Van Gogh, to escape insanity such
as this, into a serene world
of self — and not shadow of self. I shall
fly over the barnyard fence and mate with
the moon to breed a new day's sun seen in
a different setting of cloud or blue sky.

Why . . .
oh, why I'd want to look alike as all
members and think as they, escapes me and
on that note I escape. I don't want even
to crow like a rooster tiered up
on a shelf, or a perch.

# The Ruins

Let's swarm on the tourists' bus and
there discuss the strength of the
Roman arch. Ruins of prisons
seem all that remain for us
noteworthy in our country . . . stones
of Port Arthur, Norfolk, or our
Queensland's St Helena . . .

                          all else
seems hidden of our past. Prisons
are our showpieces of virtue.
Enough to make old lags scrub hard
and polish faster the floors of
stone that are their outlook now.

I wonder if these tourists are the
get of police and warders? Someone
has to lock us up here in our
history, away from ourselves?

The stone walls stand around us; our
view of beauty is the blue sky which
we stare at as at a pope's cupola
patterned with angels of our bland
imagination.

                   There's a green
growth of grass soft underfoot. How
seldom prisoners would lie upon
the sward with clover in their teeth!

Dreamer! they'd curse these grey walls down.
Must we laud jailers here for ever?

# Death

Death — not while I've will to dream is
your presence welcome; unless you
marry me in sleep. Then, and then,
my friend (already I unbend,
become familiar), welcome
at my bed . . . a pleasant greeting
and farewell.

            Such brief acquaintance
leads to make me dwell upon those
pleasantries had we two met
in youth . . . the interminable pain
and turmoil shoved aside . . . dreams
of the other side of the moon —
the coin spun in our favour.

                      They
in your care: how have they prospered
who own all the stars, the sun, the
moon and, yet, preserve some plot
on Earth — dispute the night with day,
carry all away in shadows?

Time's not to rack them on his
wheel. Space is their continent.
All dwell in levitation
of some dream encompassing
this Life whose doubt surrounds me.

# False Dawns

Waking in the early hours and
looking towards the East, not the dawn
but industries' flat low grey clouds
lit by furnaces are all I
see. Hopes for a brighter day fade.
Yet I am warned, should that mock dawn
not glow, my fate is doom. How does
the sun rise now on other worlds?
We've watched our manager, or heard
his plane take off to journeys there;
but we, on shifts, must keep the cloud
aglow, live ever here beneath
that canopy of smog, or fear
what leers above throughout the year.

## II

Starvation (we're not told) as the
old weapon of imperial
might regains ascendancy
in the tall cities which we can't
bring down as once we breached the walls
of fortresses . . . is the weapon with
which the Castle now fends off the
mob's siege. Those empty offices
our bread supports echo with gibes
should we storm their heights in comfort
of plush elevators that
mock our shacks, briefly as we trip
to Heaven and descend to Hell

## III

where through a scrappy forest of
tares and thorns steel-jawed giants are
champing diets of pulp to be
excreted as dead leaf-like shrunken
dollars. We pick up, here and there, a
few soon wrested from us by the
griffs in uniform. Here men live
uniform lives to survive; but
caught in a uniform no man
is human. His value is the
uniform's. Discard the jacket,
they'd have him skinned ready for the
coals — the obese cannibals, their
fat devours the bones it covers.

## IV

So they will devise the plans for
their collapse with ours, unconscious
of their near demise, unconcerned
at ours — the millions less? They don't
watch the census, leaving the count
of lives to lackeys . . . prefer the
'exclusive'; not to be touched by
'average man', despising the
average to which they lower him;
hating the individual
who escapes their averages.
Against that man they cry aloud,
'Democracy!' and the crowd harks,
shelters beneath the low grey clouds.

## V

Believers? Clouds (the roof of death)
they see the grey as colour of life's
ceiling; some, dreaming to be
managers in this dreary light, dig
their fellows harder, bury hopes
as the grey clouds lower every
morning. Though they build on a hill,
they look down on cloud, failing to
see Earth whose colours moulder from
the lack of light . . . only sighting
the unhealthy flush instead of
jewels which the spectrum's peacock
fan would once display in a
vast plenitude to infancy.

## VI

How shall we conquer words again?
Always new leaders choose to don
that uniform of Law and Order
and bring us to book; despise our
arts as a dangerous story
not to be told until a safe
century has passed, when we may
glorify Napoleons . . . or
Hitlers, next? But in the meantime
name him, best, eccentric who would
break the line they draw around
their game of politics — that grim,
hilarious game to them, where juntas
inconspicuously use force;

# VII

tag on their police their manners;
all persuasive of the better
life, at their elections. After . . .
the brutal bash, the stricter law
with belts to tighten and warning that
the wheels of industry are slowing.
Prayers to the clouds again for
the devout among us? Devotion
is the mood they look for from the
mob. If we must pray to the furnace-
glow on smog, these are false dawns with
fiercer hours to shape under the
hard lights that watch interiors
of factories, both night and day.

## Factory Boss

He bleeds and bleeds the countless
pale corpuscles of his sweats which,
on appearance, don't rate a glance;
but when his temper rises the
corpuscles are pulsing with the
blood's red fury.

           His anger
is immense: tall as a chimney —
stack which writes black messages of
smoke on hitherto clear skies. One
can imagine the furnaces
beneath that factory chimney . . .
but the factory doesn't
(sad to say) make ease.

           Wait for
Saturday, when the corpuscles
lose count again; he'll be content
to cool down — apparently with
not much smoke to write about his
riding the high horse.

           The winds will
have unbridled that animal
which should then be freebooting to
the country, or following a
breeze that phases out to sea.

           He'll
seem no longer the factory
boss, but recluse.

           Have they pulled down
the chimney stack?

           At least till Monday.

# Up the Back Stairs

There may be an alga growing on
our bones — an incipient stain
on our china-ware. Porcelain
crazes and may become the pattern
of an old face — a dish that falls
from the mantelpiece. Tendencies
and tenancies formulate into
tenderness: watch an old cart
stop at a new gate of unnumbered
address. Soon there is that possum-
shuffle up the back stairs and eyes close in
sleep in deference to the blind light of
the day's disaffection for love's meanings.

# The Geese
*for James Allison*


The charts by which the geese fly nights
as though there were no obstacles
in shadows are folded under-wing.

They pass over the islands
of the sunken temples where the
priests are cormorants and each mass
is solemnly attended by
the fishes.
        They carry souls by
charter — hosts on each passage which
they assuredly accomplish.
                Each
has an inbuilt compass. I
envy them accoutrements which
guide them point to point across the
lands and oceans . . .
            directions I
see as a maze and can never
follow in my groping hour by
hour of daylight.

Black out the sun
for ever, if I were gifted
with familiarities as
theirs with orbs and galaxies . . .
as though each sipped of stars all night.

Chained with them I may get drunk a
little — but have their pinions
to ferry me beyond all comment.

# Studies in Time

## I

The aged fail to pay due tithes
to Time, but stand on unguarded
bridges, unsighting dark waters,
never throwing in a shilling
as I throw in ten cents now;
though the worth of the coin's metal
is not face value, water in
the stream is polluted, there is
not a gleam of silver to be
seen. Ours is a pit-head world where
dross is recycled by miners
to whom pennyweights are now as
ounces mined in those early years.

## II

I turn out my pockets of trash, and
puzzle — have these been my counters
of Time? Was my life measured by
such meaningless tokens? What I
could barter for them now seems the
incongruous in oblivion.
This is bric-à-brac of space. In
a vacuum of emotion
am I to carry such dross and
seem the wistful soul, confounded,
upon whom men can rely?
Why have men this charge, this concern
about my person? Must I respect
such devalued coinage, buy Time?

# III

Values matter first to me. I
must see value for Time. All streams
must seem pure for my shilling.
It must shine; I must see its gleam
like a fish's, as it sinks to
the bed. I shall wait on each
bridge, passing over pay Time there
a tithe for each decade Time barters.
You will not stumble me into
drains. All along I have had a
side-eye for sharp practice. Why are
you clicking your tongue? Why are you
the impatient one selling me Time
as Progress — some boon to be bought?

# IV

I slot in with youth that seeks no
reward from a game but the play.
Such a small aperture for my
coin . . . such a spread of Time within
the machine. Eyes hang on a point,
or a number meaningless to
Progress. So many numbers may
be packed into unsaleable
Nothing. There are overtones of
Commerce and its billions that the
Press headlines into the waste bins,
to appear and reappear like the
stale names of old stars: Hope, Crosby,
Wayne, Taylor — paid with bought credits?

# V

When day stacks upon day and night
upon night their wet fusions of
greed, how shall my diary be read? Mould
lends the appearance of fur. Is
this a dozing beast, or is the
animal decomposing, dead?
Life is a lump which Time has
stumbled upon, inopportune?
Dig the grave. Cover the error
with hands over your eyes. There are
a myriad journals pulped thus each
day. Numbers are a safe escape.
Why! you couldn't read even the
title of my book. Was it Time?

# VI

If we could claw the numbers out
of space — from all gas, liquid and
solid — would they remain in each
mind, taunting us like a boy's
sums? I have a horror of them.
I dread to heed disappearance
soon of the alphabet: to have
to speak and write in them or, rather,
be dumb for ever while digits
fiddle their idiots' fingers
and I have to obey their
vagaries. A matter of Time —
Time's inexhaustible numbers.

## VII

Not one mean bracket could I claim
but my name's registered at
entrance and exit. Here I am
guest ever, one of the public
kept under surveillance so not
one could pass through with a pilfered
spoon. A great feast for the eyes, such
consternation, as the hands twitch
in emptiness. Light fingers would
try their touch, even clutch at a
straw from the packing of some plate.
They say, this was spread for Queen
Isabella of Spain; any
tarnish of banquets scoured by rub.


## VIII

Each statue in this hall has the
traditional penis and twin
testicles — left, hanging lower
as it appends in life — but the
avant-garde male in the wide
vestibule has a hole in
his guts. Kids play faces through the
space when the attendant wheels on
his heel. It's had its touched by them
all. That may have been the sculptor's
dream: to keep contact with flesh. Now
I come to remember, there is an
ancient bust of a woman with
no head, arms, limbs. How take her hands?

# IX

I think a tree touches the sky
more delicately than would
man's grab for the Heavens. I
had open eyes as a boy and
watched the congregation with their
heads bowed, eyes closed and hands held as
though for the dive. Bad lad I was
who devised pictures of the flock
in a concerted plunge into
Heaven, all too awkward and hunched.
Some, I mused, would fall back flat on
an arse, others would topple and
stub fingers. I knew that to dive
needed timing, spreading balance.


# X

'You haven't the idea of
adding sums, son. You're subtracting
from the quantum of your life. Look
upon the expanse of my
estate! Everywhere you will heed my
title to the land. The police
will show you boundaries of
trespass. I live every day
all over my estate. There
is no country left for you,
bound to the freeway on which you
must not loiter, else be as
straying cattle, soon impounded.

## XI

'Time is the computer of my
wealth, programmed by echoes which
chime with my desires. I've had sly
thoughts about a fuse, like naked
revolutionaries: these were
computerised to alternate
the circuits at will on breakdown,
so the system functions willy-
nilly, even after death. I
have the satisfaction now of
knowing the works will grind and
grind the populace into an
extinction. Computers will be
programmed to shout my name alone.'

## XII

Those views were from the Mount. When I travelled,
down blind in a basement flat below
street-level, the basic colour, brown of an
old calendar two years out of date,
I wondered who had tenanted the dive
long enough to check upon a day, a
week, a month, a year. Terrifying,
succession to such a tenancy; but
Time was humble at the door to take a week's
advance of rent without questioning. I
wondered how many needle-punctured lives
had been carried out the door and up the
steps of that death-serviced tenement, and
turned to fumble for my own syringe.

## XIII

I spoke to my dog, of other
dogs we'd met in our lane. He'd
scented each one's piss, accepted
my definition of the names
labelling each; but when I called
each dog back to memory, he
pricked his ears and opened wide his
eyes to *now*. Now was the only
Time he dwelt in. Misunderstood,
my false ideals for canine worlds that
spun on each breath for him. I failed
to recognise my crassness as
he sunk back in Time's abysmal sleep.

## XIV

Two scabrous weeks we tenanted
the limbo, until I could no
longer live within the flesh, but
felt that Time had fixed upon my
death. Even love smelt stale upon
the blankets — love that perfumes life
as briefly as a flower
then pods in seed to sow
again, but in some new-turned bed
raise the perpetual family . . .
Time meaningless in likenesses
of faces. I left an old clock
on the mantelpiece, enough the
image of my deserted child.

# Holiday Sea Sonnets
# — 1985 —

To Hazel May Triggs

# A Launching

To barter my ideas to you, I
have assembled here, my pencil, paper
and words, knowing: to clear my ports of fear
I cannot captain eyes and ears without
presence of a star: and if the terrors
of the night should cloud, I need the sound
the rhythm of the sea — mast, sail and water.
I long to navigate to safer
ports than mine. The tide, the wind, the waves
to let me know the launching's over,
the voyage has begun to other's minds.
How else to trade opinions, unload
at friendly ports the perishables I
carry in my head? How replenish thoughts?


# Wave-Watching

I watch the largest body on
Earth wobbling, yet with rhythms of
tides. So much jollity here,
that the rocks I sit upon lack.
I take enjoyment from the tumble
of waves along shorelines so
expansive an orderly pattern
of poetry's discernible;
whereas the rocks at my feet
are an image of misanthropy.
No happiness accompanied
their fierce genesis here, but
pressures. I relax by the
sea, fleshed upon Earth's skeleton.

# Surfing

I dreamt myself riding upon bubbles . . .
the foam subsided and the wave let
down and limped — a ripple on the
beach. What an exposed dank creature!
I picked my limbs up, straightened them,
assembled shape as man. Into
green, blue . . . encores again and
again, until the surf rang in
my ears, ever after hearing the
waves that washed into my sleep. A
surge I can't forget now as all
those waves ring in my ears . . . the feared
heart-pressure pent to echo in
a flood of never resting surf.


# Swallows and Seagulls

At the beach the appearance
of the swallows is not noticed
in the presence of the over-
awing naval bearing of the
seagulls; but they have a gladness
in their voices, unheard in their
nervous twittering up-town;
and, if the tight orbit of their
flight seems trivial when rivalled
by the masterful span of the
coastline by gulls, they are on the
wing ceaselessly, oblivious
to naval presence, enjoying their
cleric satin anonymity.

# Describing Crabs
*for David Malouf*

I look at crabs. I'm searching for
odd nuts and bolts; but surely life
never screwed together such a
contraption as a crab! Or did God
read Frankenstein before the book's
weird character was created?
He'd have had the novel well in
mind before He said, 'Let there be
Light . . .' or was His a slap-up job?
Having a few scraps of bone left
over from the graft of his part-
assembled universe (great leaps
between moons and planets, comets, stars)
His hands wired up these tangling limbs?


# Sonnet Like a Jellyfish

Swims like a jellyfish in a
sea of ideas, but doesn't touch
on tangibles without fatal
wreck. So has to swim among the
probabilities and, if some
colour is discernible,
is happy in that sea. Seems to
have backbone, ribs — like umbrellas
erected by jellyfish,
that assist them to take shape in
the Earth's mightiest of all
domains, except one — the mind's vast
ocean which gives scope for my
thoughts to shape this sonnet for you.

## The Couple at the Top

However high they built there was
an edge to the sea over which
they could topple. Space was not their
monopoly. Rather, space was
their prison . . . and the couple at
the top level, umpteen floors up,
slumped at imprisonment. Their
plush suite pleased only the devil.
Their roomy unit at the top
of 'Far Horizons' rising high
above the beach, didn't seem to
let them see more than the sea. They felt
cheated — each with suspicions that
the other could see further out.


## The Bony Bream

The youth with his fishing-rod that
reaches towards Tahiti, plays
then levers a tiny silver
bony bream onto the rocks. He
is satisfied raking up the
leaves of angling. A forest of
tailor once adumbrated the
waves off this headland. Shame has no
recollection of past years for
him. He didn't over-harvest
the sea. This minute silver bream
the sea has left for him — much as
winter holds one tiny tinselled
leaf, lonely trembling on a branch.

# The Mindless Ocean

Gale-haunted days which occupy
whole seas, chase bays into coves
spoiling anchorages. Our sails
trimmed mean as a spinster's skirts, the vast
mindlessness of ocean confronts us with
unknown destinations. Landfall
on reef may impede, destroy us.
Each ship must steer a course alone
when storms divide. Where leisure rode
in harbour, there is a fury of
waters without moorings; surging
currents like writhing eels that
cannot be contained, spill over
the starboard breakwater, twist out of mind.


# Mullet in a Wave
*to Rodney Hall*

Surfing, with that frieze of mullet
on the unattainable wave
that breaks beyond my powers
of swimming, I have seen the fresh
hieroglyphs of fish, spaced, yet
packed thick in the shoal as I would
expect in flat dimensions held
fast in blue dye. Hieroglyphs
of an immeasurably rich,
a priceless tapestry of the
Nile; held high in profile on jade
papyrus . . . with time for vision
of a moment to recognise
a message from pharaonic gods.

## Letter Written on a Holiday
*for Bruce Beaver*

The Pacific's a vast blue page on
which the lines are ruled white. I am
scribbling on a small sheet of blue-lined
white note-paper. I am toiling to
fill a few lines while on a beach
holiday. Each day fills in the vast
blue page with white lines of breaking
surf. My apologies — three weeks
won't convey more than this message
of goodwill to you on one blue-lined
white sheet. But please see through my words
a blue background of the vast page lined
with surf. Friendship may there ink in
lines on which these hands failed to scribble.


## Graphs of Delight

There were curves sweeping away on
missions, so definitely to
purposes: as dolphins emerge
from tangled seas, or seals in the
surf. I could imagine, lounging
at my leisure, following their
trajectories . . . pleasures of
planing birds for which the effort
of adventure was to follow
the arc of the horizon
extending vision, disc upon
disc, of the circle; spiralling
higher, higher — never failing,
faltering. Safely above Earth.

# Seagulls' Tracks at Botany Bay

A puzzle about these ivy vines —
they aren't climbing old English
manor walls; don't carry leaves
at all even in Springtime's
clean sunshine — but they link
the leaf shapes of ivy and
trail over the beach dunes where
the English first landed.

Pity for Aborigines
who'd known this pattern fifty
thousand years and didn't glimpse
portents of clinging ivy in
the gulls' tracks printing the sands
with due wariness for the English.


# Container-Ships

I'd have to be born, a little boy, again
to see for the first time ships at sea creep
over the horizon in shapes like these
container-ships to sense romance once more
traversed the oceans. Instead, in my old age,
I see a montage of these barge-like vessels crawl
into my universe, like shell-humping snails.
Their ugly boxed deck-freight piled like the
square block architecture of a modern
city to which they lug containers of
the baubles pampered civilisations
consider part of 'the good life'. Theirs now the
contours imprinted on the skies of cities
renowned in olden times for domes and spires.

## The Colour of Distance

So many miles into the mountains a
sea seems waiting above me for sight of
a cloud to sail into the deepest blue
skies. Why is the wonderful always
dressed in this unsullied blue? I gaze in
your innocent blue eyes and then I fear . . .
how far away is their love from me; for
blue dwells in distance — in the deep sea, in
the skies over the mountains. Still I would
gaze there, for my life's dreams are real. I
live no life outside my dreams though I toil
far from access to deep seas and tall skies
over mountains. Someday I'll visit all
distance, sail or soar within range of your sight.


## Mirror

Drifting over to the western
side of the lake, this seems the
only shore; although its waters
lack the turbulence of an
ocean. I sense men facing me —
mirrored quizzical visages.
A storm between us the only
insurance of that privacy
I cherish on beaches. Any
fracture of such calm poses the
unwanted. Perhaps if I climb
a hill and stare into the sky
I'll see my soul-like image —
until black clouds drift over.

## Surf-Sigh

Hush! The surf compounds all voices
day and night. The surf is somewhere
to steer a garrulous friend, to teach
him, the multitude doesn't heed him.
He has to listen to the hush of
innumerable waves on the beach; he
has to listen, or shout a shrill
monosyllable to equate the
importance of rousing seagulls.
He may get through with a piercing
shriek of his name, but only if
he calls downwind with the beach scud.
You nod back at him, ear cupped
disconcertingly deaf to him.


## The Sea

I suppose I took most of my joy
from you . . . if you are an entity
much as I hold fast to my
ego. Perhaps my great folly
my idea of inanimate matter.
Yet I know you have nourished my
life, are greater than I. Just how
can the part be greater than the
whole . . . is my puzzle, when I know
you must be eternally living,
endless and bluer than skies,
outliving man's life and, how else
can life survive without your kiss?
All reason drowns: drowning in you.

# The Nature of Water

I have a feeling of being
waters of an ocean, a gulf
of it, or a tiny vessel's
equivalent contents. So
much of matter lies in the great
oceans changing uniforms of
colour as the weather portends.

A tidal wave, or a ripple: I am
sent such messengers from the ocean.
When my flesh is reborn
as a raindrop, I shall return
in time to sea-level, lap on
seashores; wait, ordered by the
moon to carry you its message.


# Weatherman

The clenched fist battering the shore
shall change some features long before
ocean's roaring surf has lulled the
headland's rocks to sleep. How swollen,
sore, looking bruised and blistering
under a cloudless sky the black
boulders lie like heads knocked out and
slumped within a hempen square. I
see clouds gather to such brawls, and
land and sea can't meet without some
fighting. Somebody should chide them.
That referee, the weatherman,
should sail mid-ocean and hold
each fist to stay such brawling.

# Drizzle

The sea has blown in over the
littoral suburbs. Vision is
baulked beyond harbourside houses
which loom and huddle like ships berthed
in port. Sextant, chronometer
are idle implements on such
a day that has no divisions
of bells. All hours seem fluxed in
a silver diffusion. Tasks
pile unrostered. There's no motive
in action . . . just to lie on a
couch or a bunk and wait till the
sun, moon and stars stir again to
resume their points for new bearings.


# The Boat-Minded Man

The boat-minded man went sailing in his
skull in the night — that white-hulled skull of
his that shone in the moonlight and sheared five
points to larboard, lying on his hand in
bed, stopping the scupper plug of his ear.

Stars twinkling on eyelashes, bearing towards
starboard, he felt moon-slippered toes planing
the air; knew a more solid footing on
deck on the waters. Thus he sailed with
a cool head, slept through until morning when,
with pale shrouds and blankets pulled over his
head, he trimmed his top-hamper and rose
from bed furling the sails, peered through portholes
seeing a new day. I've been sailing, he said.

# Poem for Asia

I have never written a poem for Asia.
That indicates how insular poems
may be. I have written many more poems
than a thousand, but never a poem for Asia.
Once I made mention of that Continent's
vast shoulders and its penis, India,
dripping islands into an ocean; but thought
of Asia as a body not measured by roads,
without a sky over tens of thousands of
towns — just land filling Earth as spoil.
Placed there, the black hole of geography
into which knowledge lapses contritely,
crushed into one word, Asia. I have never
written a poem for Asia; now ponder how to.


# The Korean Tiger

Ha! said the tiger, the hunter is dead. That
glass-eyed head he had mounted for his wall has
told me. His rifle is old iron. In Korea
what need have I to look like the moonlight striping
the tall grasses? I have sprung from the high hills
onto the open fields. No more silly games with
the stumbling hunter. I have sheathed my claws
to pad all over the farms and roads. I lap
water from the rivers where the children trap
eels. You may see the grooves my claws rake through
the rice paddies. I have fleshed the whole land for
my people to share the prey. That is a false
fable which would tell them, 'The Korean
Tiger is extinct'. Ha! says the tiger.

# The Prey

There are wolves, bears and leopards
in the higher mountains . . . or
are they rocks and shadows of clouds?
I can imagine the ducal beasts
where mountains follow me, my day's
journey from Seoul to Kyongu . . .
those many hours winding through the
valleys where rice fields float like
lily-pads and, looking up, I see
a waterfall leap from the sky. What
prey does it fell on the heights?
Only the purest water tumbles
into the valleys from the peace that
time and beasts stalk in the heavens.


# Korean Farming Villages

Time could pass these farmers' villages
and not stop by this century.
I have seen the farmers in their
fields all day as I have travelled
with the sun, looking one side or the
other from my coach. I ask, 'Does
time need visit them as the Old
Reaper hurries me along — harries
me?' Theirs is a kind journey
from field to rug. The sun would seem
to check each hour for me, while he
ticks ages for them, passing from
his eastern to his western rooftree,
tiling night across their valleys.

# For the Young Silla Princess Whose Live Body Was Immured in the Molten Bronze of the Great Temple Bell

The trees are climbing all over the mountains
like children climbing their parents' knees. They
stand on the shoulders of the hills, making
the hills look higher. The taller they grow
the prouder their parents become. 'These are
our children,' they say. 'We shall protect
them until we may rest in their shade. They
shall hand us down from the High Temple of
Buddha the calm and peace of the little
Princess whose heart's blood softens the metal
of the Great Bronze Bell which tolls for the wise
priest at the fourth hour of each morning.' The
people in Kyongu hear of that great gong
that the Silla Princess wakes not in sorrow.

*Based on the legend of an ancient Silla King who wished to cast a great bronze bell
for the Buddhist Temple high in the mountains near the Silla capital of Kyongu.
Each time he had a bell cast it would not sound, until he ordered that his young
daughter, a princess, be thrown live into the molten metal, after which a bell was
cast that sounded.*

# At the Tomb of the Silla King

They said to me, 'Come with us to see the tomb
of the ancient Silla King.' What had I
expected . . a grotto in the hills, a grey
stone vault, perhaps a pyramid? Instead
they showed us this perfect rainbow of green grass
— a hemisphere of happy earth which
left me with much doubt that death had ever
lingered here. A world of grass for
kings in which to dwell eternally
at peace: a stable hemisphere for
one who chose to watch a constant sky . . .
who knew the many generations
of spry crickets that would live here too,
supernumeraries to the Silla King.

*Kings and Queens of the ancient Silla Empire the capital of which was Kyongu*
*(Gyeongu), at the time of the 10th Century A.D. with a population of over one*
*million, were buried in tombs beneath large hemispheres of grassy mounds. Some*
*half dozen have been opened and contained golden crowns and other precious*
*items. One tomb is open for public inspection.*

## Waiting

Thoughts of dying are drying up
sightless tears in my late years
of living when a draft of wine will lift
aeons from shoulders too bowed to load
with cares. Life is easy now without
expected industry. I ham hopes for
a few more pointless years to balance
infancy with its unknowledgeable dreams.
Colours, sight and sound still present
and, if I hear a trifle less obediently
the moments passing, that is my gain —
my neutral shield from pain at the
thrust of news. History has me somewhere
wound in an inviolable shroud, waiting.


## Then and Now

I knew the child I was. I know
the child I see; and the world is
no less wonderful to him than
the old world was to me. I
know the treasures he shan't find and
that brings sorrow to me; but he
has a new cast of mind that will
register equal glee as I knew
when my world was young, though it was
very old and scarred according
to its history. Yet love was
then as love is now, a treasure
for all time, as I have watched the
child's parents see their young child play.

# A Dripping Tap

I am told that water is so
weak and I believe description
of the fluid that washes through
my fingers like a shadow; but
moments pass, add up to seconds —
so many in an hour, a day,
a week — a lifetime and their flood
of consequence is on me, can't
be stemmed. So in old age I count them
towards my death, remembering the
drowned — an ocean's calm and silence
after a storm. Yet here I can't
conserve the dew that dries upon
the sward. Water and time flow
as a dripping tap — unnerve me.

# Uncollected and Later Poems

# The Lucky Country

Here in a wire-fenced country laced
up like a nineteenth century
beldam in tight whalebone corsets,
movement's restricted to pegged roads,
trespass an unsafe excursion;
and as most roads that would explore
all country remote to easy
access are dirt and dusty grey,
or brown gravel, or yellow clay,
or the earth's thin crust on stone
ravished by agistment cattle
that eat anything except tins
and bottles strewn among stumps of
burnt trees and white bones, there aren't
enough pedestrians to bear
the weight of flies.

                   Desperate lives
string out for miles, separating
in distant states which only a
continent relates. They call this
'The Lucky Country'; but who 'They'
are is indefinite as an odd
yard of the infinite Nullarbor,
or hour in the Gibson Desert,
or street sign on a dying star.

Perhaps we'd come across them in
an airport's bar, their bags packed and
fares paid for by the taxpayer:
the good-times politicians for
whom the 'Lucky Country' prospers
at all seasons of the year
cum flood, cum drought, cum fire, cum burr.

# At the Inquisition

Downstairs is my Queensland
house's refuge with its
cool summer's hideaway
from toil and women's talk . . .

hens and cats and deckchairs
together, without plans.
I remember here I
was not called up in the

war years: perhaps because
I was downstairs and now
declare I didn't hear
the war: perhaps because

I was dreaming in that
peace under the house
in the Country which I'd
heard said was Down Under:

perhaps because I was
dreaming of Poetry
under my Queensland
house: perhaps because I

was never asked why I
wasn't a soldier and
didn't defer to a
war which wouldn't walk down-

stairs to tell me to stir
but let history hang
itself from the joists of
my high-stumped Queensland home.

## On this Planet
*for Malcolm Blight*

The wind's eeriest trick was to
make audible, words. The silent
planets without atmospheres and
oceans would have provided us
with space which we may have occupied
as model tenants. We may
have rivalled Earth's saints there. Quiet,
in an assembly of dreams which
may have fashioned more fanciful
punctuation than flowers to
Earth's terrestrial terrors, we,
each on a dead planet with suns — all
planets mirroring reflections.

# A Pair of Shoes

Angie fetched herself a pair of
shoes: bought from Drakes, repaired
by Duckmanns. They paddled her 10
splayed toes to the Fair, but were soon
trampled by pigs that gorged upon
them and she was lucky to limp
away barefooted, feeling she
had no toes . . . stiff, as though her bare
ankles were crutches, and she winced
at the angle of each step throwing
weight upon her crushed coccyx while the
crowds hung on. She could hear them at
the Fair: guffawing, chortling at her
back. She felt for many knives
aimed at her back; but a mass of
people is innocent she knew, so
she watched the sky to see whether
the sky was raining knives and 10
pierced her body . . .
                                but the heavens
were blowing only kisses and
an occasional sigh — which may
have been hers. She had no doubt
the pain was hers. Even a hedge
she edged near scratched her face to
prove that the pain was hers. She knew
so much pain dammed in her body
and mind and the mind's pain hadn't
begun to stream out. Her moaning
was merely that dam's overflow.

She had to burst out crying and
you could see the pain flooding
out through her eyes from body
and mind . . . but even the trickle
of the crowd leaving the Fair
didn't wish to ford a stream
of tears to wet their best footwear.

# Outpatient

As I watched them come in for their deliveries
(impersonal as postmen, these women) I
thought, not irreverently, of bundles . . . bags;
yet recalled to mind, I was not delivered
by some meteor, some princely avatar . . .

saw here, all was as common as life: the skimpy
total of possessions each woman seemed to carry
externally, as though life had returned to a
pristine existence however plush the home a
woman deserted for this fountainhead where
fundamental waters sprang — as at some spa
where one may hope for health, an elixir.

I, with the worm in me, the outpatient who had fear
of the crab instilled within my psyche, sitting
on a bench biding the nod of Nemesis.

Oh man born of woman, I reproached myself,
where is your vaunted strength, your fortitude?
Here in the gut-realm of the hospital, you are
not the master. Here the newborn will be God
or Goddess over you, to numb your nerve, to
shackle you forever to all human kin.

# The Bone

I have a bone and all dogs chase me.
I flee with ears like cherubs' wings on glee's
shoulders: so fast my feet pace past
in a wizard's whirr and the dogs string
behind me like a comet's tail. I
have a message and everybody
wishes to halt the messenger charged
to effect swift delivery.

I will not drop the bone at the feet of
you, master. The chase continues with me
in possession. No dog bothers to
count the nine points. The chase continues.

Until I drop the bone, contention
will divide the pack. I'll be threatened,
but known as the dog that stole the bone
a head's lead from the mongrel horde. If
I am caught I shall race at the flanks
of another hound. Nobody will
carry the bone to his threshold to crunch.

Too many contend to deliver the
message which hasn't been savoured by
anybody except the wind. Keep up
or you'll not stand a dog's chance. Cliches
will hinder you. You will forget the chase
which is an important link in the
chain of events. Dogfights divert
those hounds that have fallen behind the

pack. A cherub's wings favour the scroll
tied with ribbons and sealed with a prophet's
kiss. All is anonymous as a bone
fliched from a prophet's tomb by feral
beasts. It is white. I have it, cannot
stop to appraise it. The chase is all
that assures me of its merit.

# The Sunflower

I miss the sunflower which the
day should place in a blue sky, this
fog-grey winter morning. So I
shall stay in bed and wait upon
the hour for its cloud-buried seed
to burgeon with its golden bloom
I know will shine again on Earth —
a light of cheer afforded from
this single source . . . unlike the night's
pale lily moon and violets
of stars beautiful but lacking
warmth. Instead, a flower larger
than a dinner plate heaped with lush
serves of sunlight for a frozen me.

## Seagulls in Moreton Bay

A string of beads of seagulls with
their quick eyes, red ruby beaks dipping
at the water's edge along a
leeward beach rippled by the squalls
that skip across this landlocked bay
of islands, Moreton Bay, with all
the barefooted alacrity
of footloose urchins skylarking,
while picnickers stay indoors, lose
a day. I am the explorer
who would have reigned discoverer
of a pristine scene to whitemen's
eyes two centuries ago, when
on such days gulls aligned these shores.

# Faces in a Crowd

When I peer at faces in a
crowd I see experiments on
person. Never the same contents
in each visage. Possessed by angers
in unripe infancy, in age
a play of demons. Faces pass
by in a crowd, but always one
by one I see each countenance
searching for the harmony that
I seek in myself. Stare in the
mirror as I may, I see my
imperfections acting grace in
age . . . then patent flaws. I smile; so
acquiesce in others' defects.

# In Brussels Square — September '85

Unlike the journeyman, the soft
poet views the Square unmindful
of the Guilds which solemnly met
here teaching the craft of masons
who, at heart, were artists — never
set-square architects building a
tight square. The Square isn't square
though facade faces facade round
a cobbled place which footsteps smooth
and polish as a tide its floor.
Four centuries now the moon has
lit the Square over the scalloped
skyline's silhouette — here, unscared,
stray cats on slates midst chimney-pots.

# The Angels of Rome — September '85

Rome, city of angels who are now
petrified in stone, or fading
in frescoes, posed in paintings; yet
mingling in the streets I glimpse a
living semblance; though denied her
wings, innocent and unhurt. I
lose sight of her in the restless
throng which treads the cobbled roads
following old ways — footprints on
footprints decaying as old leaves
providing nutrients for the
ever-present, ever-lasting
City that cannot be destroyed,
but grows eternally upon itself.

# Cosmopolitan London

I saw London so late in life!
Somewhere in a closet I hid
the Globe's Map on a ball-size sphere
I used to spin, neglecting its
earnest study. Sufficient the
British Empire stained its surface
red at every tangent and
History was Geography. Pass
one subject and I was passed in both.
Then came Singapore — *Renown* and
the *Repulse* sunk within the
hour. The waves closed over British
glory — my Globe was valueless —
Now the Empire lives in London.

# One Wintry Friday Morning

The sun was lazy up this morning. It
had a bank of cloud to hurdle before
it could colour the world I inhabit.
The winter threatened snoring like an idle
dog ignoring burglary of my house;
but a lazy sun woke and as I looked out
I could see the jewels of the Bay, and
the cloudbanks materialise into the
colourful offshore islands with their
sandblasts like solid lava of sunshine.
Otherwise, and the day had been grey as
army blankets, as thin and cheerless rags
to be pulled up to my chin in chagrin
at another day wasted — so few left.

# Walking to the Cow-bails — Mid-winter 1931

At 4 o'clock, one winter's morning, my
shadow lay upon the ground, subdued and
shrinking from a chilly night and cowered,
so seemed, by an accompanying giant
which towered above me, steel-grey ghosted as
a mist-born shadow menacing my life.
I coughed. We three in Time pressed on towards
the waiting herd that comfortably chewed
cud in the enveloping dark; each beast
guarded against the Devil by its horns.
Then, in my lonely youth, I pondered my
place upon an alien Earth and held
the lantern fast against these weird creatures,
that other shadow belonging to this hour.

# Echo

My mother introduced her to me in
a railway subway at Wynnum South. 'A
young blue-eyed woman,' she said, 'chained within
the subway walls!' and I have heard ever
since her muffled sad response to diverse
utterings assaulting silence within
compounding walls; be such in a valley's cliffs —
death's grimmer boundaries. Never she escapes;
and I have aged to know my dead mother
in me, plays her part. I hear her echoes
in my every poem. I walk with
Echo in my saddened heart, because I
know the spurious walls, supposed, are real
and wish she walked again to break their seal.

# Greenway Street

I live in a one-way street and turning back is a hazard, so
my autobiography will never be written, few memories kept.

The street circles the knoll of a hill. My house rides the collar
and the knoll wears a crest of trees of the original bush
        that pokes
through civilisation as though true Earth were about to raise its
head to gaze upon desecration.

I fear I see only the thinning hairs on its head. These are
stringybarks losing their sap and leaves, standing sparse as hair
iron-grey in death's desolation. So I've seeded the knoll with
acacias, shortlived but flowering to excite pleasant comment. I
listen to the hill's ideas.

Sometimes I cross the street to pull weeds, where the
        forest cover
is balding and sun encourages scabs on nature, such as
        rattlepod,
stinking roger, natal grass — raspberry red and known too as
railway grass.

There are no trains here. All transport's pedestrian, or veering
towards that ideal. You'll notice, I haven't to walk a straight
road to eternity in search of reasons to confirm my philosophy.

There are no signposts of a beginning. My street leads the
        path to
ever, if you set out to walk its way. Nobody sees the end to it
        when
they enter, unaware of my house's number; but my view is to
        the east

where a ribbon of sea is discernible on a bright morning
      — even ships
that sail among blue clouds of islands.

That makes a happy frieze on the edge of my day: ships
      sailing in
seas of islands — suggestions of escape, or arrival.

I am happy at home — happy to know that the sea is not drained
yet and islands are still afloat as clouds.

My hill is an island.

I wander around its street, happy this loop on my hill holds fast. I
meet myself often when I stroll; but like the hour hand
      of a clock
always as I am, never as I was.